What Others Have Had to Say About Tony Galliano and the Impact of This Book

"In The *60 Second-Strategist*, the author deals with a broken kid's life story (surf loving) that made millions in his life time. This is something like Tom Cruise's *Mission Impossible* movie. It's a thrilling, fast moving picture of that individual. Tony Galliano also nicely presents the success stories of various individuals and fresh thinking processes needed to get financial freedom, by changing life style and ways of thinking.

This book is relevant in times of economic recession as well as prosperity. Tony has written with his good experience and provides the reader with practical tools and suggestions to achieve success.

The young kid's career transformation to a financially independent person is nicely sketched in The 60 Second Strategist. At times, I felt like I was reading a *James Hadley Chase* novel."
-*Ravi Bhaskaruni, TechMahindra*

"After receiving Tony's 60 Second Strategist I instantly devoured it in one sitting. Not only was I able to gain insight into my business but also my life. His experiences and professional advice has been an asset to me till this day."
-*Kelsey Bratcher, Infusionsoft*

"Tony, just wanted to say 'thank you.' You really broadened my vision far beyond what I thought possible. I would caution anyone thinking about working with you who is also comfortable with the status quo to be prepared to have their world rocked. To be candid, you also surprised me in that you didn't just play the role of 'helpful visionary guy,' but also focused me on the wealth of details required to execute the project."
-Greg Silverman, President, Silverman Solutions

"Tony's combination of experience and expertise makes this an excellent resource."
-Jennifer Rush, MABC, CEO, IQT2 Corporation & Empowered Learning Solutions and Faculty at Axia College of the University of Phoenix

"The book is very simple to understand and entertaining. A very good resource for those always in a hurry." ...I liked it."
-Alex Almeda, Pragmatic Quality Advocate, QU Guild

"Great Book..."
-Daniel Medeiros, YouProduct

"Tony has been very helpful in helping a lot of my physicians as well as my staff become familiar with new processes and ways of thinking and doing things.'"
-Dr. Jeffery White M.D., White's Pediatrics

"Tony is very forward thinking and has given Whitech some very innovative ideas that we really plan to implement... and his energy is high and he is very creative"
-Clara White, CEO Whitech Electronic Medical Records

"More than a book about business strategy, this book has practical applications for overall life strategy"
-*Leslie Peterson, Twenty Million Angels*

"Personal experiences shared to the readers... gives us a lot of examples and ways to deal..."
-*Pratyush Agarwal, Sr. Software Engineer, Zensar*

"Irresistibly clever and inspiring – a must read for everyone in business."
-*Julie Tyson, Sheboygan Press*

"The use of examples makes the book worthwhile to read and to think about the cases being described. I liked it a lot."
-*Joe Essers, CNO at Manifold Management International*

"I have been going carefully through your... insightful remarks and suggestions. I am sure they will help me, guide me and strengthen me in my future work."
-*Dr. PJ George, PhD, Editor and Textbook Author*

"The book is very simple to understand and entertaining. A very good resource for those always in a hurry." ...I liked it."
-*Alex Almeda, Pragmatic Quality Advocate, QU Guild*

HOW TO TAKE DECISIVE ACTION TODAY WHILE PLANNING FOR TOMORROW

TONY GALLIANO

SIXTY SIGMA
CHICAGO, ILLINOIS

This publication is designed to provide accurate and authoritative
information in regard to the subject matter covered. It is sold with the
understanding that the publisher is not engaged in rendering legal,
accounting, or other professional services. If legal advice or other
expert assistance is required, the services of a competent professional
person should be sought.

Library of Congress Cataloging-in Publication Data

Tony Galliano

> 60 Second strategist : how to take decisive action today while
> planning for tomorrow / Tony Galliano

> p. cm.

> ISBN-10: 1-4392-2536-2
> ISBN-13: 978-1-4392-2536-3

> 1.Strategic Planning. 2.Decision Making planning.
> 3.Strategy   4.Title

Library of Congress Control Number: 2009900375

Printed in the United States of America

CONTENTS

"There comes that mysterious meeting in life when someone acknowledges who we are and what we can be, igniting the circuits of our highest potential."
~Rusty Berkus

Some Important Acknowledgments

YOU **MUST** READ THIS!

I have been blessed by the influence of some of the greatest minds in business, government and academia, each and every one of whom have helped me bring my dream from concept to reality. To them I am pleased to extend special thanks - they all were major contributors to my business success and the development of *60 Second Strategy*.

I owe a huge debt of gratitude to . . .

Brian Tracy for inviting me to co-author the *Wake Up... Live the Life You Love book with* **Wayne Dyer** *and other great people.* Without Brian's "jump start," I would never have become an author.

Dan Kennedy for finally getting it through my head that nobody in business cares about my education or pedigree. Okay, Dan, I get it... By providing extreme value to my clients, I don't need to rely on certifications or degrees.

Bill Glazer, my marketing coach, for helping me cut through the garbage and get some of this knowledge I have stuck in my head, into a useable format that can actually be put into practice.

Lee Milteer, my personal success coach and author of *Success Is an Inside Job*, for teaching me to believe in myself and my business to the extent that failure is not an option and extreme success is the only end state for me.

Charna Halpern, Improvisation Coach and CEO of the iO (formerly Improv Olympic) for teaching me the power of teamwork under pressure and how to develop the intuition to react at lightning speed, bypassing the need for cerebral thought. It's no wonder Charna made stars out of Mike Myers, Chris Farley, and Tina Fey.

Congresswoman Andrea Seastrand for believing in me when few others did and teaching me to stand up for my convictions at all costs.

Chris Pontius from *MTV's Jackass* for challenging me and getting me to think outside the box... WAY outside.

Prince Saeed Muhammed Abdulahi aka "Jabu" for teaching me straightforward honesty is always the best policy.

The late **Tim Hall** of the *Oakland Raiders*, for showing me how to passionately follow my goals and to never back down in the face of opposition.

Marvin Ellison, Executive VP of US stores for **Home Depot** for showing me that you can make it to the top and still always maintain the highest integrity.

Steve Warshaw, former CEO of *Chiquita*, for all those late night chats at the bar where he taught me how to set and maintain a vision for a global enterprise as well as preparing me for the flack I would later face for choosing to do the right thing.

Anne Cooney, VP of Power Division at *Siemens* for finally getting it through my thick head how brutal things can be at the top, and for mentally preparing me for a level of corporate warfare I never knew existed.

Professor Rich Makadok, PhD from *Emory University* for teaching me to understand 376 pages of strategic thinking documents in 24 hours and for honing my diagnostic reasoning skill to bring my thinking ability up to the next level.

Patricia Hermann of *Hermann International* for the gift of *Whole Brain Technology*, and for teaching me how to dramatically tap into my intuition in order to help other people and organizations achieve.

Professor Ricardo Court, PhD, for bringing his experience from UCLA, Yale, Fairfield, and UW Madison to encourage my study of business history which brought the *60 Second Strategist* concept to reality.

Major Kyle Crawford, US Army, for teaching me the human side of military strategy and how to apply leadership concepts to any situation, both on and off the battlefield.

Katherine Rockefeller for teaching me that American Aristocracy is still often noble and classy, regardless of what the media would have you believe.

All the **ER physicians in Rome, Georgia** who spent all those years with me… helping me understand intuition and action under pressure. These guys apply the 60 Second Strategy concepts every day in real life and death situations.

Professor George Easton, PhD, from **Emory University** for sparking my interest in Six Sigma, process capability, and statistical process control which eventually led to the foundation of Sixty Sigma Inc.

Peter Jatreboff, Executive Director, *Morgan Stanley,* for his true inspiration on what an individual can achieve before age 25… and 35… and willingness to be my Manhattan Role Model… even if he is 2 days younger than me.

Neuroscientist, Dr. Pavel Jastreboff (Innovator of the Jastreboff method of Tinnitus treatment featured on *Good Morning America*) for finally getting it through my head that I know absolutely nothing. The more I know, the less I know. I never knew someone so brilliant could be so kind.

Most importantly, my wife, Leslie… for believing in me and my dream. Without her, none of this would be possible!

So, you stuck with me through these well deserved accolades and recognition of many outstanding relationships (many of the names you probably know), so if you're convinced now that I just might know what I'm talking about, let's get going.

By the way, if you ask half of these people about me, be sure to use my birth name, *not* Tony Galliano. I changed my name after this Psychopath murdered his pregnant wife and dumped her body in San Francisco Bay. We shared the same name and I got sick of the publicity. If you don't know who I am talking about… GOOD. IF you don't understand why I would do this, try getting strip searched by a TSA agent twice a week at the airport because, according to your ID, you are supposed to be on death row…. But I digress!

It's time for you to become a *60 Second Strategist*.

Introduction

"They say it takes a lot to win ... and even more to lose."
-The Grateful Dead

These days, many of us are re-defining what it means to win.

Our over-busy lives and a fast-paced 24/7 world place many demands on us in "the here and now" and at a very heavy price. That price is our future. Workers around the world are literally being eaten alive by the pressure of balancing daily responsibilities, short term demands, and long term goals.

I should know... the stress landed me in the ER... three times, and the operating room once. There's nothing like a stress test on a treadmill, staring at a mortality chart, to give you a little life perspective.

So, what exactly is this 60 Second Strategist book about anyway?

And why would I open a strategy book with a quote from a rock band?

Is this just another gimmick of outrageous claims in a feeble attempt to sell a book? You tell me.

Is it a gimmick when an ER physician can re-start your stopped heart in less than 60-seconds?

Is it a gimmick when a US Army Infantry squad can clear out a terrorist hideout and secure enemy prisoners without sustaining a casualty... in less than 60-seconds?

Is it a gimmick when a team of fire fighters enters a burning house on the brink of collapse and rescues a trapped family... in less than 60-seconds?

60 seconds is a lot of time if you train your mind and body to react quickly, efficiently, and effectively.

So maybe, just maybe, you can trust me to teach you, as I have taught so many others... how to accelerate your thinking and organize your daily actions in a unique way that will dramatically improve your business and your life.

Keep reading and I will show you . . .

. . . how to manage your daily priorities while setting aside time, energy and resources that focus on the future. If you want to be truly great, to live a great life that is fulfilling and healthy, you **must** find a balance between planning and execution.

To do this, you will have to get a handle on your life and learn to speed up, automate and delegate much of your current daily routine. I will show you how to do this.

Proactive vs. Reactive

The speed comes from developing what are called, *Diagnostic Reasoning Skills.* Sounds complicated but it's not. Much like an ER physician or combat soldier, you will learn to react at the speed of light to more than 90% of the daily situations you face because you have proactively learned the skills taught here. This will free your mind to focus on long term objectives... the stuff that really counts. No more drowning in minutia.

Most business strategy books focus on organizational, or "high level" strategy, which is great. I teach workshops and consult at that level all the time. This book isn't about that. This book is about *you!*

The fact is, if you can't manage your own life, career, and daily routine, you are going to have a real hard time taking care of anything else or anyone else. For a team, business, family, or organization to be forward thinking, strategic... and all that good stuff, the members of the team need to get their house in order first.

So how do individuals and organizations become more strategic? How do they become great? How can people become more innovative, intuitive, and creative?

Well, sorry to say, there is no single "magic silver bullet" that does it all. If someone has sold you that kind of solution, go back and get a refund ASAP! The only thing a silver bullet is good for is killing vampires, and if vampires are your problem then this book is not going to be much help.

I have been studying this strategy stuff for a long time. You could say it's my life's passion. As with most solution-based philosophies and concepts, it was born from a mating of desire and desperation.

I started writing in the journal which eventually became this book in a motel room in Seligman, Arizona, way back in August of 1993.

That's a REALLY long time ago, isn't it? Fifteen years and counting.

Point is, this isn't some hastily pieced together book filled with worthless clichés and mind-numbing figures used as filler so you'll experience a good "thud factor." In fact, I have tried to make this book as short as possible.

I actually want you to read every word of what I have to say. To take something important away with you.

Over the years I have isolated a few hundred strategies, tactics, principles and techniques that lead to the ability to execute effective strategy quickly and effectively. In this book, I have narrowed it down to sixty. Instead of giving you a big list, I have followed in the wisdom of the great teachers of the ages and show examples of each principle in a story format. Not just any old third-hand story, but stories from my own experiences.

You're going to come along with me and peer inside my mind like a CSI as this whole "60 Second Strategist" thing grew from concept... to a business and life-altering toolkit for those who use it properly.

Everything presented here is left-lane fast paced. If you are expecting a Sunday drive or some pap designed to just make you feel good about yourself, put this book down now and go read a John Grisham novel.

But if you stick with me, you will gain insights on how to implement powerful strategic thinking principles. I'll show you some specific examples of how this stuff can work for anyone.

There are tools in this book that you can use today. Forget the hype, fluff and filler.

Your life is waiting for you NOW. You don't have time to mess around.

Do you?

Let me address the beginning *Grateful* Dead quote by telling you, It DOES take a lot to win. You will have to stretch outside your comfort zone. You will have to take risks. You will no doubt fail one way or another during the process. You wouldn't be human otherwise.

So yeah, it takes a lot to win. Dang Skippy.

But remember, it takes even more to lose. Losing is costly. The 'Dead' got it right (as rock lyrics often do). More on that later.

On this journey we'll call "Becoming a 60 Second Strategist," you might occasionally get frustrated, confused, or discouraged. That's okay.

You might try a new idea and have it blow up in your face. That's okay.

You might invent a new product and not sell a single one. That stinks, but it's still okay.

That's life and it's how things work. You have to get up, swallow your pride and get back in the fight.

When you are down, always remember one thing: It costs 100 times more to lose than it does to win.

"There are few sorrows, however poignant, in which a good income is of no avail." ~Logan Pearsall Smith, "Life and Human Nature," Afterthoughts, 1931

Sure, it can be tough to tear your business, your job and your life into tiny pieces. It can be frustrating to examine, restructure, and reprioritize everything.

You will be tempted to give up and just throw in the towel. That's when it becomes crucial to examine your thinking and approach.

What will your life be like five years from now if you don't tough it out?

Where will you be? Same job? Same income? Same lifestyle? Perhaps you will even go backwards.

It has happened to me, so I know.

When I look back at the days following when I got laid off, I remember how hard it was. I was scared out of my mind. I was humiliated. How could I explain to my friends, family, and professional network that I was unemployed?

I had thought I was invincible. After finally becoming an executive, I had thought that only people from the "labor force" were vulnerable to downsizings, right-sizings and other such sizings. I thought I had finally escaped my past. My mind flashed back to my humble beginnings as a homeless, first generation American.

I thought my years of clawing my way to the top had finally brought me security. I thought my fancy MBA and Rolodex of powerful people made me immune from my trials of the past.

Boy, was I wrong. After teaching and coaching strategy to executives for all those years, could I actually use this stuff myself in an extreme crisis?

Sure, my strategic system worked in the military, sales, marketing, coaching, operations, and several other "organizational" contexts. I was able to make it to the top once before, but what about now?

How could I support my wife, who was paralyzed from the waist down from a car accident?

How could I feed and clothe my four kids?

How would I pay the mortgages on both my houses?

I was scared, even paralyzed with fear (sorry, Leslie). Around the same time, excessive stress lead to health failure. Like I said before, I went to the emergency room three times.

One ER visit landed me in the operating room. I almost died during the surgery.

Almost dying has a way of giving you some perspective. Near death, as they say, is nature's way of saying, "Hey, stupid, pay attention!"

Now, when I look back at my life like the roiling wake behind a boat, and then look at my freedom today, and examine the impact I have been able to have on others, I can't help but realize the cost of giving up would have been 1,000 times greater.

It would have been MUCH easier for me to just become a local consultant, or call up some classmates from business school. These guys are executive level managers with companies like Coca-Cola, Home Depot, Siemens... you get the picture.

Instead, I chose a different route. I chose my family and my health over going back into corporate slavery.

I have over $1 million worth of training and coaching in my head (and I have the receipts around here somewhere to prove it).

Instead of helping another billion dollar brand become a two billion dollar brand, I decided to apply these "well kept corporate secret strategies" to my own life and teach others to do the same. Put *my mouth where my money* is.

This decision has already put me in the firing line. One global corporation has sent multiple "cease and desist" letters to my home, claiming that the strategies I teach are confidential.

What are they afraid of anyway?

I admit that much of what I share with my clients (and now with you) falls under the category of "well guarded secrets," but none of these secrets is "company confidential." In fact, I discovered that one company's "secret strategic process," is also "secretly" shared by nine out of ten Fortune 100 Companies.

So now these corporate types are running around with their hair on fire whining that I am a thief or a criminal or something. Are they so terrified of your success? Are they so frightened of their 'secrets' being discovered? Or do they just know that you may be coming for their jobs? For their corporate jet? For their home in the Hamptons? They remind me of the schoolyard bully who turns out to be a coward when confronted with boldness.

It's kind of hard to ignore all that bluster but remember…

It takes A LOT to win!

But when it comes down to it, you have no choice but to win. Losing is unthinkable.

The cost of losing is almost immeasurable. The cost of losing is a life unfulfilled, or in my case, a life almost lost.

Can you bear the cost of staying in a job you hate?

Do you want to bear the cost of looking into a loved one's eyes and saying, "I can't give you what you want …or even worse …what you need…"?

So what's it going to be?

Are you going to be a LION or a LAMB?

Will you join me and the ones who came before me and shared what they discovered? Will you use this growing body of knowledge to improve your life and your business?

Do you want to better the lives of your loved ones, and positively influence hundreds …thousands …or even millions of people?

Or will you stay safely on the "easy road" and settle for mediocrity? One of my favorite Bible quotes is:

"Enter through the narrow gate; for the gate is wide and the way is broad that leads to destruction, and there are many who enter through it." Matthew 7:13

Will you go through the wide gate and settle for less? Would you rather happily crash in front of the TV, be oblivious, and let other people dictate your life?

We both know the answer, right? If you weren't motivated to change things you wouldn't be reading this book, so …

Let's get into the battle together and kick some butt.

"Money is better than poverty, if only for financial reasons."
~Woody Allen

Becoming a 60 Second Strategist requires hours of preparation, so let's get to it!

DO THIS NOW

1. Go to www.60SecondStrategist.com and take the strategy assessment quiz to get a baseline of how good your strategic thinking already is.

2. While you're there on www.60SecondStrategist.com register for the FREE *60 Days to 60 Second Strategy* Online Video course.

Chapter 1

"Don't Chase the Wrong Waves"

"Dude, why did you go for that wave? I have bigger waves in my bathtub. Next time, wait for the sets to come in."
-As told to Tony Galliano by Chris Pontius from MTV's 'Jackass'

Much of this section was inspired by my pastime as a foolish surfer wanna be. More about that later...

Naples, Florida has to be one of the most *beautiful* places I have ever lived. Perhaps second only to its neighbor, Marco Island, Florida... the most *peaceful* place I have ever lived.

If you have ever been to these places, you might think that money actually does grow on trees. Palm trees. There is so much wealth there; it's enough to make you puke green with envy. But stick with me through this book and you won't need to be jealous of anybody. They'll be jealous of you.

When I first moved to Naples, I actually thought that Bentley must have started a line of cheapo cars. Why? How else could one out of every 20 cars on the road be a Bentley? I went to the dealership and checked it out. Sorry folks, they still cost $300,000.00.

Anyway, when I first moved to Naples, I just rented a small villa in a nice gated community called Pelican Marsh, right across from the Ritz Carlton. I was doing a lot of work commuting between Florida and Chicago, so the family stayed in Chicago.

I ended up spending more time in Florida than in Chicago with my family, so I eventually brought the gang down with me. The villa was too small, so we started house hunting. Sometimes life can be like a game of Dominoes.

I never REALLY paid much attention to the Naples area until I committed to moving there. Then I made a startling discovery...

There's A Whole Different Planet Out There That Has Yet To Be Fully Discovered-

But put away your telescope - you won't find this one in outer space ...

It's called planet "Disgustingly Rich" and it's inhabited by people who collect million dollar homes for a hobby, like the little plastic ones in Monopoly, and buy a new 50-foot yacht every other year. I mean, who wants last year's yacht, right? (Maybe those tone-deaf auto executives who flew to D.C. in their luxury jets to ask Congress for a bail out!)

Listen, everything we believe about money right now is nothing more than what we have been programmed to believe. Let the un-programming begin right here.

"Money will buy you a pretty good dog, but it won't buy the wag of his tail."
~Henry Wheeler Shaw

My house hunting adventure led me to meet a man named Pely. Pely was a young immigrant, no older than twenty-five.

One day, a friend told me that this Pely guy might have some property on Marco Island I'd be interested in.

The conversation went something like this:

Me: Dave told me to call you to see if your property is still available.

Pely: Which one?

Me: The one on Marco Island.

Pely: Which one?

Me: Dave said you had one on the water ...on a canal with a yacht lift and a pool.

Pely: Which one?

Me: He said you currently have it listed for $1.5M.

Pely: Well, I have two houses that fit that description. Why don't I give you directions? They are both already fully furnished and move-in ready.

Me: So, when should I meet you?

Pely: I'm kinda busy today ...you can just let yourself in. I never keep my houses locked. I mean, if someone needs the furniture that bad, they can have it.

I really liked both homes, but decided on the one with the bigger pool. It turned out Pely owned over a dozen million dollar homes in Naples, Miami, and Cancun. Pely told me that he decided to move his family from Miami to Marco Island for a better quality of life. He started doing some remodeling to the house I'd decided I didn't want.

I watched the renovation progress on a regular basis, as I used to pass by his house on my morning jogs around the island.

One day, the house was gone. Completely demolished! I called Pely to ask what happened, thinking it may have burned down. Pely told me that he got frustrated with parts of the remodeling project, so he decided it would just be easier to demolish the house (mid project mind you) and start from scratch.

I should note that Pely wasn't even a real estate investor. Real estate was more of a hobby for him.

Guys like Pely aren't even "Rich" by Naples standards. In fact, 400 of the Fortune 500 CEO's have homes in Naples. Talk about money.

I quickly learned that I was definitely an "outsider" in Marco Island for two reasons:

1. I was the only guy in the neighborhood who went to work in the morning.

2. I was the only guy who did not have a 50-foot yacht parked in the canal behind the house.

I felt "equalized" after Hurricane Katrina swept across the island on its way to New Orleans and capsized my neighbor's yacht. Their weeping echoed across the canal as their yacht was dragged away in pieces. You'd think they would have insured the thing...

Why would they? The "disaster" was the perfect excuse to buy a new, bigger, and even better toy.

I think the one characteristic the super affluent people I met shared was that money just wasn't a big deal. I'm not saying that they are necessarily complacent. I mean that they just look at money like most people would look at dog food or dish soap. Money and the toys it buys are everyday commodities that really aren't anything special.

Money may be the husk of many things but not the kernel. It brings you food, but not appetite; medicine, but not health; acquaintance, but not friends; servants, but not loyalty; days of joy, but not peace or happiness.
~Henrik Ibsen

Over the past few years, I have had the pleasure of meeting several Internet Millionaires. They seem to like me better when I hide my education and corporate background. In my more ignorant days, I regarded their style of marketing as tacky, annoying, and unprofessional. Then I saw how they actually live, work, and play. These guys are for real.

Imagine Frank Kern, an ordinary guy from Macon, Georgia ...who organized the StomperNet launch which totaled over $24 million in sales in just a matter of days. This made me wonder: Was I truly considering *everything*, or was I placing snobbish limitations on myself.

These days, huge Internet product launches, from INDIVIDUALS, NOT BIG COMPANIES, are becoming more commonplace. As of this writing, Rich Schefren recently launched a coaching program which reportedly sold over $981,000 in just two hours.

What's my point?
You can accomplish just about anything - including the impossible - if you want it bad enough.

Success breeds success. I truly believe you ARE what you pay attention to. It's called 'paying' attention for a reason! Do you want money? Do you want more quality in your relationships? Do you want to help people? Pay attention! In other words, focus on what you want or want to accomplish, for what you focus on is what you'll get.

If you believe it can be done, then go do it! I have seen proof all around me. After being surrounded by so many millionaires, corporate CEO's, and celebrities, I remember saying to myself, "Wait, I'm smarter than that guy! I'm better educated than her! How come they have everything they want and I don't?"

Then I figured it out. It took years of research, but I finally figured it out. And you will soon know it too.

It all goes back to my teen years when I was learning to surf.

I lived in the middle of nowhere, outside of San Luis Obispo, California, which made life pretty lame growing up. When I turned 16, everything changed. I became the proud owner of a red Datsun 210 Station Wagon...with a primer brown hood (no, that was not considered cool in my neighborhood).

I saved up my money from my paper route to buy a cheap used surfboard in junior high, but never got to use it much because I could never get a ride to the beach. Now that I had wheels, it was time to get serious about surfing, so I tried to follow my friend, Chris Pontius, around to get some "cool surf tips." Years before he became a star on MTV's 'Jackass', Chris was just a normal guy, just like everyone else. In fact, some considered him a lesser human being than everyone else. Let me explain.

Chris and I met in fifth grade at a special magnet school for gifted students. We were in little league together; I even gave him a kitten once when our cat had a litter. His dad was a cardiologist and his mom was a college professor. Since Chris lived out in the sticks like me, we became instant friends and hung out quite a bit. We would spend the night at each other's houses and sometimes go on overnight trips to places like Disneyland.

I'm sure Chris' dad was the only cardiologist in town who let his kids build a skateboard half-pipe in his yard. I am even more certain that Chris was the only doctor's kid with TWO half pipes in the yard.

As a teenager, my mom saw danger signs I couldn't and she forbade me to hang out with 'creative' people like Chris. Yes, if you have seen 'Jackass', I'm sure many parents would do the same. The part I find interesting was my mother's dire predictions about the future of "those Pontius kids".

While traditional parents forced their kids into educational straight-jackets and rules and "fitting in," the Pontius parents were different. Despite the fact that both the mom and dad had a PhD and MD respectively, they believed their kids could be successful in whatever field they chose and taught their kids to believe in themselves, not goals set by others.

What was the result? Chris is a rich and famous "Jackass" (a very happy jackass) and his brother, Matt, is a professional skateboarder (a very happy skateboarder). They both followed their dreams and found the pot of gold. Not bad for kids who grew up 'in the middle of nowhere'.

Perhaps I should have skipped business school and pursued my original dream of being a lion tamer. I guess it's never too late. How much do lion tamers make anyway?

But back to surfing...

When I started surfing seriously, I tried to make it out to the beach every day. In fact, after my mom left town and abandoned me with no place to go, I wound up homeless at age 16 and lived in my car. Guess where I parked at night? The beach.

Why? Because surfing rules!

The term 'surfing' conjures up images of idyllic days in the sun, glistening bodies and warm Pacific waves, but that image belies the reality of the sport. It's one of the hardest things you can ever do. After a day on the water, in the water, and under the water, you feel beat up, like you went a few rounds in the ring with Mike Tyson! This is not a joke. I have competed in dozens of sports and have even run an ultra-marathon (33 miles), but nothing compares to the physical exertion, exhaustion and brutality that defines surfing.

I think back to the advice I got from Chris... So many years ago:

"Next time, wait for the sets to come in."

In a nutshell, the "sets" are the big waves, the ones worth riding.

He taught me that the waves you DON'T take are just as important as the ones you DO take.

You see, actually catching a wave is a lot of work. You have to paddle your butt off to get positioned for the wave to "catch" you. Also, depending on where you are, you may have to fight off LOTS of competition for the right to ride that perfect wave.

Your competitors are often bigger, meaner and faster than you. They may have more experience, or just be more gutsy and daring.

It's really rough out there. "Locals Only" isn't just a brand name, a regulation, or saying. For some it's a way of life and even death.

So anyway...

Even if you take the silly little easy waves, you still have to work like a madman to catch them. On top of that, the "ride" they give you is mediocre at best. Then you have to claw your way back into position just to have a chance to catch the next one.

Sometimes you just have to chill out and focus only on the best waves FOR YOU, not necessarily the biggest. Sometimes patience and some judicious selection pays off.

Why?

One of the hardest lessons I ever learned was on the famous Bonsai Pipeline.

When I was in college, I got a free flight to Hawaii via Air Force transport. I was in the National Guard which entitled me to fly stand-by anywhere the Air Force flies ...which is pretty much everywhere.

I wanted to live out a long-time dream of surfing the Bonsai Pipeline on the north shore of Oahu. But there were a few obstacles in the way of my dream.

First, I didn't live in Hawaii. Then thanks to the US Air Force, I overcame that obstacle, but there were still more. I wasn't able to bring my surfboard because it was in California and I flew out of St. Louis. Not many surf shops in St. Louis. There were little kiosks that rented surfboards in Waikiki (on the south shore), but not on the north shore. For those of you who don't know, I think the record wave on the south shore occurred in 1972 when a storm surge caused a tsunami about 13 inches tall.

A slight exaggeration, but the fact remained that the south shore had smaller waves than Lake Michigan. For those who doubt me, this is an open invite to surf the Kenosha, Wisconsin waterfront next summer. Send pictures.

I desperately NEEDED to get to the north shore.

Adding to my problem was that (at the time) you needed to be 21 to rent a car and I was only 19. To make matters worse, the Oahu bus system did not allow surfboards on the bus and the trip was WAY too far to walk ...especially carrying a surfboard.

I decided to go see the Pipeline first hand anyway, sans surfboard. After getting off the bus, I was disappointed to find ONE lone surf shop at the bus stop. This was it? Where was the fanfare? Where were all the pros, photographers, and girls in bikinis? The Pipeline was supposed to be a surfer's paradise. No trash talk, no hype. Just serious surfers doing what surfers do best.

After watching the waves for a few minutes, my whole body was screaming for action. I just HAD to go out on the water. I had a little room on my credit card, so I headed back to that lone surf shop to see if maybe... just MAYBE there was a cheap used board I could buy.

WRONGO, dude!

The cheapest used board they would sell me (and it was a total piece of garbage) cost $900.00. In retrospect, perhaps the $900.00 would have been a sound investment.

Back to the drawing board ...so to speak.

I went back to the beach and just watched the waves... totally mesmerized.

Then I had a BRILLIANT idea!

I decided to BODY SURF the Bonsai Pipeline. Why not? I used to body surf all the time at home. Okay, usually I would use a body board, but is that necessary? I mean, don't penguins do it all the time? ...or is that sea lions?

Anyway, I found an area with no other surfers (I didn't exactly want an audience if this turned out badly, nor did I wish for some Hawaiian local to mow me down with his 13-foot long-board) and started swimming out to where the REAL waves were. **[Note to self: if you're about to do something and there is no competition, always question why.]** After painstakingly swimming for 20 minutes, I reached a cool "shelf" in the ocean. Although I was over 100 yards from the beach, the water was only ankle deep.

I jumped off the 'shelf' and continued swimming for deeper waters. I am a very strong swimmer, but fighting the waves was a KILLER without a board to float on.

Finally, after what seemed an eternity of swimming, I saw the "perfect" swell approaching and moved into position.

As the wave grew in the distance, I could "feel" it calling my name. It grew bigger and bigger, closer and closer.

I clearly remember thinking; *this is a killer 6-footer! No wait! 8-footer! No wait! 12-footer!*

"This is it, the ride of your life," I told myself as I turned toward the shore and began swimming as fast as I could.

For a brief moment, I felt nothing... just a floating feeling as I was drawn into the wave... I felt a sense of peace and tranquility all around me.

Then, I felt the power and fury of nature as never before as the wave violently sucked me inside. There was then a brief period of being held prisoner (very much against my will) inside a very, very tall wall of water. As I began to panic, I was rudely reminded that people aren't meant to breathe water.

I was then hurled over the top of the wave ... you'd probably say I was exaggerating if I told you I was hurled 15 feet straight down. I couldn't tell you for sure... I didn't have my tape measure with me, but it felt like 50 feet.

Have you ever done a belly flop off a high dive? Hurts, doesn't it?

That doesn't even compare with the pain I felt at the bottom of my fall. Remember that "shelf" in the water I mentioned earlier? Well it turns out there's LOTS of them on the Bonsai Pipeline.

They are not made of sand.

They are not made of stone.

They are made of razor sharp coral formations.

Yes, that perfect dream wave slammed my body down onto a coral reef. I was in too much shock to feel the tiny jagged edges of coral slice through my skin like thousands of tiny razor-blades.

I began coughing the salt water from my lungs and gasping for air. I looked behind me and saw another wave... an even bigger wave, headed straight for me.

Nowhere to run... nowhere to hide... I lay back down on the reef, hugged it tightly, and braced for impact.

CRASH!

Wave after wave, beating after beating, the barrage continued. I was 100 yards from the shore. The waves were so close together that I didn't have time to "make a mad dash for the beach" between the sets. Besides, I was scared that I would just smash into another reef. I was scared, disoriented, and thought I might die.

The next day's headline would read: MORON DIES IN LAME ATTEMPT TO BODY SURF THE PIPELINE!

I began to recall the stories of how surfers have been pulled under water and trapped in the little caves that formed underneath the reef. Great. Another way to die. The only thing missing was a twenty-foot shark and with my blood in the water how far away could that be? Amazing how terror brings such moments of clarity.

For the next 30 minutes, I endured the beating. Wave after wave crashed into me as I hugged the jagged reef. After deciding that the waves would never ease up, I let one more wave crash me into the reef, then I made a mad dash for shore.

I didn't look back, I didn't slow down... I put every ounce of strength I had left into a sprint that probably broke some kind of speed record.

I was still 50 yards from shore when I felt a powerful wave suck up my weak body.

I must have done ten summersaults in the water as the wave crashed down. I was trapped in the whitewater and tumbled over and over. I couldn't even tell which way was up. It was like being in a big commercial sized washing machine and I couldn't reach the 'off' button.

I remember kicking and flailing as I gasped for air. I said a quick prayer of repentance (for being such an idiot).
I knew then it was time to meet my Maker. I just hoped He didn't count off for stupidity.

In the distance, I heard an angelic voice say, "Laddie! Laddie!"

That's when I really panicked! I wasn't ready to see "them pearly gates!" I kicked and flailed even harder.

Again I heard, "Laddie! Laddie!"

Wait a sec... the voice sounded Australian. St. Peter wasn't an Aussie ...was he?

I heard the voice again, this time it was SCREAMING!

"LADDIE! LADDIE! STAND UP! STAND UP!"

So I did.

Much to my surprise, I was actually drowning in about 18 inches of water.

As the Australian lifeguard approached me, I walked to the dry sand and kissed it ...eternally thankful that I had lived to touch terra firma once more.

The Aussie put his hand on my shoulder and asked...

"What the heck were you thinking, Laddie?"

"I dunno," I said. "Where were you anyway? Aren't you supposed to be saving idiots like me?"

He said, "Yeah, but I was too busy saving that girl over there that followed you into the water. Besides, I could tell you are a really strong swimmer, am I right?"

Suddenly full of pride that I had survived, I casually bragged, "Yeah, I have surfed a bit and I swam and played water polo in high school."

"Well, you're lucky to be alive and that girl is even luckier!" he exclaimed.

It turned out that she was from Oklahoma and had never even seen an ocean before. She figured it was safe to swim ...because she saw me do it.

As the Aussie turned away, he pointed to my chest and said, "You might want to clean that up. If you don't, it will get infected and can scar pretty bad."

I looked down and saw my ENTIRE body was covered in blood. The coral had literally sliced thousands of tiny cuts all over my chest, stomach, legs, and arms.

After washing my cuts out at the public shower, I passed out on the beach from sheer exhaustion.

I woke up with the worst sunburn of my life. I was as sliced and red as raw sushi and couldn't move for two days...
So, what's my point?

Surfing IS JUST Like Business!

Sometimes you will be more successful by saying "NO WAY!" Than by saying "yes".

Here's what I mean: There's opportunity EVERYWHERE so you have to make judgments.

Every day, I am pummeled with new opportunities to make money.

When I first started out on my own, I seized on an opportunity to do a project for a huge international client. I was sick and overburdened with existing work, but took the job anyway. The project almost sent me back into the hospital.

The next week, I got an invitation to take part in a major project for Motorola.

Was the project worth a lot of money? Yes!

Did the project have potential to lead to more work? Yes!

Did I take the project? NO!

It was not in line with my personal goals and the direction I was taking with my company and my family life. It wasn't easy to do the first time, but since then, I have learned from turning down several big opportunities. I have seen my "almost" partners make tons of money from projects I have turned down.

But you know what? That's okay. If you spread your focus

out in too many directions, you'll be like I was as a 16-year old beginning surfer. You'll waste your energy chasing after garbage.

If you are doing something that gives you success, keep doing it. It's much easier to do what you are currently doing and do it BETTER than to move on to the next big thing.

Also, be careful of the "next big thing," or "the next big wave," because it can kill you. Success isn't found in chasing little waves or big waves. It's about catching the wave that's "just right!"

Oh ...and be careful not to follow someone without getting the facts first. "Miss Oklahoma" almost killed herself by blindly following me into the ocean. A simple conversation with me would have told her that:

1. I have several years experience in the water and have swum competitively

2. I am a trained lifeguard

3. I grew up with Jackasses like Chris Pontius and will do lots of stupid things on a bet, whim, or dare.

4. I plan on writing a strategy book in several years and I need an anecdote to showcase what complete and utter stupidity looks like.

"Miss Oklahoma" also taught me that no matter how dumb you are... there is always at least one person around that's dumber than you.

And with that thought, I give you a 'Yogi-ism' just for fun

"A nickel ain't worth a dime anymore."
~Yogi Berra

Your 60 Second Strategy:

Eliminate Distractions

By

- Managing your time so you can focus on long-term goals rather than routine daily activities

- Keeping stress in perspective and preventing emergencies from derailing long-term goals

- Regularly challenging traditional methods of thinking

- Not letting your daily schedule interfere with long-term thinking

- Reserving time and energy to contemplate and act strategically

- Finding a quiet place to think that is free from distractions, interference and business
- Identifying "waves" in your work; map out strategies to manage them

- Developing the discipline to control mundane activity straps and firefighting

- Periodically weeding out unimportant tasks and obsolete responsibilities

- Develop techniques to control internally created "waves of distraction"

DO THIS NOW

1. Go to **www.60SecondStrategist.com** and download the Chasing Waves strategy worksheets.

2. Identify your top ten habits, tasks, and pressures that prevent you from acting strategically.

3. Rate the difficulty you will have attempting to control these "demons".

4. Develop a plan to deal with each of the difficult distractions.

5. Ask yourself: Is there any "wave chasing" I can delegate?

6. Ask yourself: Is there any "wave chasing" I can eliminate completely?

7. Ask yourself: Are there any waves I can just plain ignore?

Chapter 2

"Locking In On Your Target"

"So, tell me what you want, what you really, really want..."
-Spice Girls

"GUNNER!"

"MISSLE!"

"TANK!"

"TANK! I said TANK! What's wrong with you? Don't you see it? Soviet T-72 Class! Eleven O'clock! It's right there! ... No, from MY position!"

BOOM!

Target destroyed.

"Sorry, Sir, I just didn't see the tank," Specialist Jacobs apologized as he took off his helmet.

"It's okay," I assured him. "It's just a good thing this was only a simulation. That tank would have gotten us for sure! Let's re-load the program again and take it from the top. I hate to get "old school" on you, but next time I have to take control of the missiles and kill the tank from my position ...I'm gonna make you drop and give me a hundred pushups. Got it?"

In the Infantry, simulation was part of the job. A BIG part. You did the same stuff over and over and over. We practiced thirteen battle drills. You had to know them in your sleep... ambush, bunker assault, react to contact.... This way, when the moment of truth came, you just had to react. The script was programmed into you. In battle, you really don't have time to contemplate things. You need to know your role and the role of your team. No time for second guessing or mistakes. Training - repetitive training - muscle memory takes over and you simply perform the task quickly, without having to think about it.

As a mechanized infantry platoon leader, I had to assemble thirty men from all different kinds of backgrounds, levels of education, and degrees of intelligence... then heavily arm them and trust they knew what to shoot at and when to shoot it. As long as everyone understood their **target** and their **role**, there were no problems.

In many ways, the so-called "dumb" soldiers were often the best ones. They learned their part and played it on cue. It was usually the "smart", clever ones who tried to over-analyze everything and second guess direction. They often thought they were "smarter" than their commanding officer. Those who could maintain a laser sharp focus on the goal at hand and not be distracted by over-thinking were the best soldiers.

When I was patrolling the minefields along the Demilitarized Zone (DMZ) between North and South Korea, knowing that there were at least ten missiles, guns, or cannons pointed at me at any given moment ... I preferred to be surrounded by focused, dedicated people over smart, clever people.

After much observation, I have come to the conclusion that people accomplish significantly more based on pure focus over clever strategy.

What? Isn't this book supposed to be about strategy? Shouldn't we all be looking for ways to be clever and such?

I guess that depends ...Is your goal to be clever, to preen and display your brilliance like a peacock, or is your goal to actually accomplish something?

If your goal is to succeed, and to become a *60 Second Strategist*, read on ...

Perhaps one of the best personal examples of goal setting can be found in the chapter that I contributed to the #1 Best Selling Book series, "Wake Up: Live The Life You Love!"

My co-authors, Brian Tracy and Wayne Dyer, definitely enjoy better name recognition than I do, but I still believe my contribution has a great deal of value and applies to the messages imparted here in this book.

The following is an updated excerpt from "Wake UP: Live the Life you Love":

Living in the Now – Tony Galliano

TAP! TAP! TAP!

I was startled from my slumber as the policeman beat his flashlight against my car window while commanding, "You can't sleep here!"

At the not-so-tender age of sixteen, I found myself living in a dilapidated Datsun station wagon, having been abandoned by my mother. She had lost her job and moved 200 miles away to find better opportunities. She didn't need a troublesome teenager dragging her down I suppose, so I was left pretty much to my own devices. Looking back, I was probably better off this way in the end but it didn't feel good at the time.

My estranged father was continually hospitalized or incarcerated throughout my teenage years. His minor crimes such as driving under the influence, and drunk and disorderly conduct, eventually led to more serious offenses like aggravated assault.

As his health and mental capacity deteriorated, my father became increasingly violent. He finally went to prison for holding a woman hostage at gunpoint during a drunken rage. After his parole, he claimed to be rehabilitated, but continued to suffer from numerous psychological and physical disorders, including multiple chemical dependencies, cirrhosis, chronic depression, ulcers, blackouts, and dementia.

Where did life go wrong? It wasn't always this way. As I pulled out of the abandoned parking lot in search of another place to sleep, I thought back to my earlier childhood.

I was identified as "gifted" in second grade and was enrolled in a special accelerated program in my school district. I was later placed in a magnet school where I learned that I had a special affinity for math and science. After completing all available math coursework, my junior high school provided me with a university math professor to build my skills; that led me to enter the California State "Math Counts" competition.

In high school, I was very active in Key Club (Lieutenant Governor of the California-Nevada-Hawaii District), Junior Statesmen of America and Astronomy Club. In addition to competing in three sports, my academic ability placed me as a National Hispanic Merit Scholar. I felt driven, to prove that I was more than the sum of my parts; that I could achieve in spite of my family and circumstances.

Then suddenly, as I saw my world crumble around me, I decided to take charge of my life, refuse to play the victim, refuse to be shoved around by inner demons, and start *Living in the Now!*

I was determined to survive so I worked at an oil refinery by day and washed dishes by night. Through a combination of night school and community college, I received my high school diploma by age eighteen.

I then received three scholarships (no way I was going to college without financial aid), which funded my first two years of school at Kemper Military Junior College. I embraced *Living in the Now* by getting involved in every activity possible including: marching band, concert band, small-bore rifle team, drill team, campus MP, and Pershing Rifles Military Fraternity. I also held leadership positions as a platoon leader, ROTC training officer, band officer and was selected to join the prestigious Scabbard and Blade Military Honor Society. Even though this might sound driven, I knew that my inner demons and my family circumstances were not in charge - I was. I was merely using them as fuel to blaze my own trail. I was *driving*, not *driven*. There's a huge difference. [Take the 60 Second test at www.60secondStrategist.com to see if you are a *driving force* in your own life, or if you are *driven* by someone or something else!]

After junior college, my father's health worsened, leading to his death. I was left to handle a mountain of debt as well as support his new family who depended on his disability income for support. After just over a year, I was able to close out the estate and help the family get on its feet. Even then I was utilizing (perhaps subconsciously) the strategies I'm revealing in this book.

Eager to make up for academic time lost while working, I completed my undergraduate degree in seventeen months at Wichita State University, graduating Cum Laude, while still working over twenty hours per week. During this short time, I was elected University Ombudsman (third in student government chain of command), competed on the varsity crew team, and served on multiple university committees.

Next came a stint serving my country as an Infantry Officer in the US Army. After sustaining multiple injuries, I received an honorable medical discharge from the Army. Using the disciplinary and organizational skills I acquired as a military officer, I found immediate success in the corporate world. I have noticed that many soldiers who rotate out of the service fail to capitalize on their experience; that's a huge mistake in my opinion.

In my first seven years, I received six meritorious promotions into positions in leadership development, sales, and marketing. I also became the second youngest graduate in the history of Emory University's #6 ranked Modular Executive MBA program.

As I launched several multi-billion dollar health care products into the marketplace, I made an amazing discovery: Most people do not have the ability to change behavior, **even when their life depends on it**. In fact, 90% of patients receiving bypass heart surgery *do not change their lifestyle* after the surgery, even knowing that their lives depend on it. Similar statistics are true for people battling cancer, diabetes, high cholesterol, hypertension (blood pressure), obesity, and HIV.

Thus began my quest do understand why it is so easy for me to achieve my goals, yet so many others equally capable struggle to do the same. I do not share this information out of any desire to boast, but to convey the fact that what I have done - the things that I have accomplished and have helped others accomplish - can be replicated **by you**.

While collaborating with Dr. Goutam Challagalla (Georgia Institute of Technology) on a project, he recognized my passion for research, my thirst for knowledge, and my quest for understanding, and he introduced me to many prominent research leaders from top institutions around the world.

My hard work and research finally paid off when I was asked to design the marketing leadership development curriculum for Abbott Laboratories. My team was able to work with superstars like Seth Godin, Keith Ferrazzi, and Philip Kotler, to name-drop a few...

But that was then...

I didn't go too deeply into the concept in the "Wake up: Live the Life You Love" book, but everything I ever accomplished was through direct **goal setting** and extreme **laser-like focus**. Sure, I like to brag about how clever I am, but in reality my cleverness usually gets me into trouble instead of helping me. It's focus that saves me!

And sure enough, somewhere along the line, I hit a snag.

Perhaps it was in business school where I was edu-ma-cated on *proper* - or what my peers considered proper - goal setting techniques.

Have you ever heard of setting "SMART" goals? SMART goals are:

Specific, **M**easurable, **A**ctionable, **R**ealistic, and Time-Bound

Well, let me tell you about **SMART** goals. It reminds me of a story my dad told me as a kid (in one of his rare, lucid, sage moments):

Dad: Did you hear about the latest research project at the university?

Me: No, what is it?

Dad: Well apparently, they were trying to breed an abalone with a crocodile.

Me: Is that a fact? So what happened?

Dad: They were trying to make an Abadile, but just ended up with a "Croc-a-Bloney"

Me: (groan) Ahh, Dad...

And **SMART** goals are just that: A CROCK OF BALONEY!

Why?

Because the "R" in **SMART** ruins the whole thing!

The second you are *"realistic"* with your goal setting is the second you settle for mediocrity. 'Realistic' is code word for 'okay'. Just like 'try' is a code word for 'it's okay to fail'. Don't 'try' - DO! Don't be realistic. Be BOLD.

When I was a sales manager, I had my sales representatives set a **BHAG**. That stands for **BIG, HAIRY, AUDACIOUS GOAL**. More than one of them got an all-expense paid reward trip to Hawaii by thinking this way. Another often said corollary is **GO BIG OR GO HOME**.

If you have been setting **SMART** Goals, I urge you to wise the heck up and throw them out right now and replace them with **CLEAR** goals. We cover this in detail in my workshops, but here is the shorthand version:

What are **CLEAR** Goals?

1. Creative, Innovative and outside-the-box

2. Linked your personal values and life objectives

3. Energizing and Motivating

4. Actionable

5. Results driven in a way that provides value to you and your organization

Here's a perfect example of how I met a **CLEAR** goal where being "SMART" would have failed me:

One of the goals I set as a homeless teenager was to graduate from a top ten MBA program. I allowed myself to become distracted by several factors, but eventually I started getting back on track. I was living outside of Atlanta, Georgia at the time and did not wish to relocate.

The problem was that there was no "Top 10" MBA program anywhere near Atlanta ...or was there? After some research, I discovered that Emory has an EXECUTIVE MBA program that was ranked #6 in the ENTIRE WORLD, not just the US. (Bonus tip: Dig deep. Don't just skim the surface. Some of the best treasure is found in deep waters, camouflaged from casual discovery.)

I don't remember the exact class profile, but (as I recall) the typical student in the program was a senior executive who is forty-five years old and earns over $300,000 per year. Not your typical iPOD carrying, jeans wearing, backpack schlepping student.

At the time, I was still in my twenties and barely earning six figures. I had no special connections and I was not a senior executive, but nevertheless I wanted IN this program. Remember, I was driving, not being driven. If I had set a **SMART** goal, I would not have even bothered to apply because it was unrealistic, but I did ...because I was supremely motivated and not deterred by so-called rational or conventional wisdom.

Two years later, I became the second youngest graduate in the history of the program. The youngest guy in the program was also in my class. Pete may have been two days younger than me, but was WAY more successful. Pete owned an IT consulting firm he started straight out of college. This guy had his own consulting firm located in Downtown Manhattan with thirty employees when he was only twenty-three years old! Now granted, Pete is a total genius, but I believe that his mindset drives his success more than his mind.

Incidentally, the oldest graduate in my MBA class was Pete's father, Pavel. Pavel is a brilliant neuroscientist ...I believe Pavel now has two doctorate degrees, at least three masters degrees and a few bachelors degrees to round out his resume.

I guess it stands to reason that a brilliant neuroscientist would know how to train his own mind to be successful. It's only logical that he would teach his son to follow in his genetically enhanced footsteps.

Your 60 Second Strategy:

Lock in on your Target

By

- Working and thinking DAILY to CREATE your desired future

- Setting specific goals that will make you more productive

- Regularly seeking to discover new ideas in your work that lead to breakthroughs

- Being ready to seize new, unexpected targets of opportunity

-]Researching and brainstorming ways to add more value to your work (not more time)

- Creating a strategic purpose for **everything** you do

- Defining specific ideas, decisions or actions you will pursue

- Choosing a goal that you are truly passionate about

- Making sure your objectives are CLEAR (Creative, Linked, Energizing, Actionable, Results)

- Being sure to **aim** before you **fire!**

DO THIS NOW

1. Go to **www.60secondStrategist.com** and download the *Locking on Target worksheets.*

2. Take a look around you. Look at the "big picture." Set the direction you want to go and specifically define the results you want.

3. Define two or three target areas of your life and your

business that you want to work on. Your laser-like focus is key to your success.

4. Determine which focus areas will yield the highest return on your energy and your time.

5. Keep an eye on factors that are changing or may change in the future that are crucial to your success.

6. Gain a specific, clear picture of what you want.

7. Make sure all of your goals and objectives are **CLEAR.**

Chapter 3

"Get Smart"

"Learning is what most adults will do for a living in the 21st century."
-Sydney Joseph Perelman

I love comedy.

Always have and I hope I always will. I was that sarcastic guy in school who always had something sardonic or mocking to say about everything. I guess you could say

"Witty" was my middle name. The term 'smart alec' also comes to mind.

Something happened along the way, though. Somewhere between my 5th or 6th corporate promotion, I decided it was time to grow up and be serious about life. Business school made me much more stern and much less funny. People in business school tend to take themselves *very* seriously, and I was no exception. Business is serious, right? Making money is dang serious business and we better get about figuring it all out. No time to say 'hello' 'goodbye', we're late, we're late, we're late …..

Losing my sense of humor happened so gradually that I never realized it had left the building with Elvis until one day…

I asked my wife if she thought I was funny. She just stared at me with a confused look. She was afraid to answer.

I turned to my four-year-old son and asked, "Is Daddy funny?"

He looked at me even more confused than my wife.

I re-phrased the question, "Do you think I'm silly?"

He just looked down and started scooting away from me.

In an attempt to make a joke, I said, "Tell Mommy that I'm silly or you're gonna get a spanking!"

He cried. My wife left the room to go and console him. Nobody thought my joke was funny.

After apologizing to everyone, I realized that I needed some serious comedy therapy. My funny bone was on life support. Fortunately, I lived in Chicagoland at that time... the international home of comedy. I think humor abounds there because when you're freezing your butt off you need a good laugh to keep your blood moving through your veins. Anyway, I Immediately signed up for improv classes at Second City (training ground for John Belushi, Gilda Radner, Bill Murray, Eugene Levi, Martin Short, and a bunch of other certifiably funny folks). Maybe I could resuscitate my poor dying funny bone.

I also signed up for classes at the iO (formerly The Improv Olympic), where stars such as Mike Myers, Chris Farley, Tina Fey, Amy Poehler, Andy Richter, and Tim Meadows got their starts.

To make sure I really got the message, I also signed up for a class at Chicago Comedy Sportz. This is where you learn quick wit "short form" improvisation as seen on the TV show, "Whose line is it anyway."

Did I mention I love being self-employed? It's nice to have the freedom to start taking a bunch of classes on a whim. It's probably not necessary to mention that I never do things in small doses - go big and all that ...but I digress...

The comedy training was great, but the best parts of the classes were the people I met and got to interact with. I took classes with Shakespearian actors (most of whom were unemployed), trial lawyers, small business owners, and college students. A, shall we say, diverse group. Too bad none of those future GM, Ford and Chrysler CEO's were there; they might have learned the meaning of comedic irony.

I love the conversations these people have. As different as these people are, it seems that most people are victims of the same brainwashing. Here's a conversation I overheard between two fellow improv students between classes:

Jared: How's it goin', Amy, you look a little tired today. You aren't quite yourself.

Amy: Yeah, I'm a bit worn out. I've been studying all week for mid-terms. I can't wait until I graduate.

Jared: I know what you mean. I'm glad those days are over. Now I can focus on getting a job. I had a great interview last week, but haven't heard back from them.

Amy: Really? What was the job for?

Jared: Delivery driver. It's kinda weird that they haven't called back. I mean... I have TWO degrees from LSU. What more could they want?

I was totally taken back!

This guy has two college degrees and can't even get a job delivering groceries! Then I thought of my friend Sean from one of my other acting classes. This guy also has a degree and is truly one of the most talented actors and improvisationalists I have personally known.

Yeah... Sean has a job ...serving coffee at Starbucks. His big complaint is that he can't get enough hours at work to pay his rent.

After hearing story after story of these struggling actors, lawyers, and business people, I started getting depressed. My wife asked me why I had started cutting classes. The truth was:

COMEDIANS DEPRESS ME!

These guys are brainwashed just like everyone else out there. Please escape! Hopefully, it's not too late for you, because:

IT'S UP TO YOU AND ME TO SAVE THE WORLD. IF WE, THE STRATEGISTS, THE RISK TAKERS, MOVERS, SHAKERS, AND PEOPLE WHO GET STUFF DONE ...STOP ...IT'S ALL OVER!

As a nation, we'll be totally hosed. No joke, man. We don't need no stinkin' cape or tights either, just some good STRATEGIC thinking.

Here are some really big problems with our current thinking:

1. It's perfectly normal to spend $40,000 a year for four (or more) years ($160,000 total) so your kid can get a degree and therefore (hopefully) get a job that pays $30,000 a year. There is a very great chance that the kid may not secure that golden $30,000 job and will have to resort to serving coffee or delivering groceries.

2. "Normal" people erroneously believe that if you get a degree, then you are somehow ENTITLED to a job.

3. "Normal" people honestly believe that you need to have a "normal" job. They do not believe this is the equivalent of tying a 500 pound ball of molten hot iron around your neck. Sorry, folks, but being "normal" is just the opposite - it's just plain insane.

This is why it's up to us master strategists to keep doing what we do. We need to keep creating products, starting businesses, and generating ideas. If we don't create value, who will?

So, am I knocking education? Absolutely not! If you recall, earlier I stated that I have over $1 Million of education in my noggin. Did I pay money just for the sake of paying money?

Heck no!

Every piece of knowledge I have acquired through education was purchased very deliberately. When it comes to my education, I spared no expense. This isn't about being cheap or thrifty, or cutting out education to save a buck. It's about common sense. It's about getting value for your money. And it's about putting the knowledge you gain to work.

Erroneously paying a single dollar for a book, class, or seminar is just plain foolish unless you firmly believe what that book, class or seminar will teach you has value. You need to ask yourself, "Do I really need this? What's this going to do for me? How will I use this?"

PROPER EDUCATION IS WORTH TEN TIMES THE STICKER PRICE.

The key word there is "proper".

One of the proudest days of my life was the day I got accepted into the executive MBA program at Emory University. I called all of my friends and family to spread the good news. When some folks found out that I was going to pay over $100,000 for a 20-month program, people thought I was insane!

At the same time, I had a friend who started an unknown, no-name MBA program. He thought I was crazy to spend so much money and was quite proud of his cost savings. His program was less than $30,000. He also bragged that his teachers were "real world" business people and not some "ivory tower" professors who have never been in the trenches of business warfare.

Two months after my program started, I got promoted as a direct result of the program. The $100,000 investment ended up paying for itself in two months. Since then, the program has paid for itself several times over.

As for my friend …He was a sales rep in a small town in Alabama when he started his "discount" education. Seven years later, he was still a sales rep in a small town in Alabama.

Same job. Same company … and completely miserable.

So much for the "real world MBA" he chose to pursue. It's all about value and worth.

I can't over-emphasize the educational component of strategy. Ignorance is the #1 killer of success. You have to know the world in which you operate and really develop an intuitive understanding for the things that are happening around you.

One of the most effective ways is by getting a personal coach. If you really want to be successful, I can almost guarantee that you won't be successful without a coach … or at least a friend who can fill that role. Coaching is the intuition side of education. Coaching is focused on you so you can focus on your goals.

A coach is someone who asks questions more than gives answers … they know how to ask the 'smart' questions as well as the 'dumb' ones. Picking the right coach may be one of the most difficult things you ever do and one of the most important.

CHOOSE A COACH, BUT CHOOSE WISELY.

Who is the greatest basketball player of all time?

Michael Jordan.

Who was one of the WORST basketball coaches of all time?

Michael Jordan.

Who is the greatest golfer of our time?

Tiger Woods.

What is the name of Tiger Woods' coach?

Hank Haney.

When did Tiger Woods face one of his biggest personal slumps?

When he went without a coach.

Does that coach have value? You bet your putter he does.

Tiger believes in coaching so much that he even has multiple coaches. Hank is just his *swing* coach. Just because the coach isn't a former Master's Champion doesn't mean he isn't the best swing coach in the world.

I could pontificate for days on the deeper meaning behind the five questions I just asked, but perhaps it would be easier to share a tale from my personal experience.

As I stated earlier I take multiple comedy classes at the top training centers in Chicago. A huge component of becoming a great actor, comedian or improvisationalist is finding a coach. You learn how to be good by taking classes and performing, but you learn how to become great by finding a great coach.

I thought I knew it all, then I met Charna Halpern.

Charna is the most amazing Improv coach I have ever seen... no wait... Charna is one of the best coaches of any kind I have ever seen. She is very unassuming... and most people have never heard of her, but perhaps you have heard of people she coaches... Mike Myers, Tina Fey, Amy Poehler, Andy Dick, Tim Meadows, and the ever popular Tony Galliano (Hey, that's me!).

Charna is the CEO of the iO (formerly improve Olympic) comedy club in Chicago and inventor of the "Harold" style of long-form improvisation. She is one of the busiest people I know because comedians, actors, and even large corporations see the value of her intuition and coaching expertise.

Charna helped Tim Meadows become a famous comedian and actor. So now that Tim is rich and famous, should we all flock to him for coaching and advice? Probably not. I only met him briefly once... and he was kind of a jerk. He's a funny comedian, but I don't think the *Ladies Man* has half the patience of Charna, nor should he.

Get it straight. Actors Act. Coaches Coach. Don't hire an actor to be your coach.

Get it?

I have been coaching people as part of a job for over fifteen years. Let me tell you that coaching is the most difficult simple task you can ever do.

One of my favorite jobs in the corporate world was coaching senior executives who had much more business experience than I did. They were extremely savvy, educated business professionals who knew the magic of coaching was not in the "business" experience of the coach, but in the "coaching ability" of the coach.

If you need information or technical expertise, go hire a consultant or subcontractor. If you want to grow YOURSELF, go get a coach.

When I first struck out on my own, I decided to hire a well-known Internet guru to help me fine-tune my company and my business model. I told myself, "This guy has made millions on the Internet; surely he can help me do the same."

Boy, was I wrong …For several reasons.

Now, I have to be careful here, because I don't want to upset any "gurus" out there and step on their toes.
I do want to be fair to you and let you know that just because someone made a million bucks on a business does NOT mean they can teach you to do the same.
In fact, chances are that they WILL NOT be able to teach you to do the same.

The problem is that the guru can only tell you how HE (or she) made his (or her) million bucks. He can show you how his systems and processes worked for him and show you step by step how he did it. There are two fundamental problems with this.

FIRST, just because it worked for HIM does not mean it will work for YOU. We all have different thought processes, different values, and different learning curves. A coach will adapt the methods for you; teach you the way to succeed. Not teach you the way someone else succeeded.

SECOND, this guru is also selling his "system" to 234,319 other people who also want to become millionaires. Do the math. It just won't work. Sure, they'll tell you that most people don't apply themselves and it's not the guru's fault if you screw it up. You must not have effectively used what you learned.

The fact remains ...if you do the same thing everyone else does, you have a very small chance of success, regardless of how good the information is.

Okay, so after dealing with my frustration with the first guru, I went to another one... and another and another.... It turns out that these people are fantastic at what they do; they are just bad coaches and bad teachers.

I wish I was just being critical ...I really do. The thing is ... these guys violate all the fundamental rules of coaching AND adult learning principles. I have spent years designing corporate coaching and training programs ... and I can tell you that 90% of the gurus out there do not know how to train or coach people. Teaching (which is what training and coaching are) is its own unique skill set - talent - and some people have it. Most don't. There is VALUE is being a good teacher. There is also value in being a good internet guru, but the two talents don't necessarily coexist.

These guys are good at one thing:

SELLING **YOU** STUFF! A lot of it, stuff you don't need, can't use, or is wrong for your business.

Okay, so I got frustrated with the one-on-one coaching type stuff and started doing group coaching.

WHAT A CROCK!

Now, I am a fan of REAL group coaching and truly believe that it has some distinct advantages over individual coaching, but much of what I have seen advertised as "coaching" is not coaching at all.

Think about this: Can you picture the coach of a football team who spouts some new plays out at his team and leaves the room and never even shows up to a game?

Kinda stupid, huh?

If you join a coaching program where you do not have a single opportunity to interact with the coach **on the field of battle**, you are not in a coaching program. Feedback in real time is CRUCIAL to the coaching process.

If you can't interact with your coach in any way, you are not being coached. You are just buying information from someone. You are being lectured to. And that's fine if that's what you want and what you're paying for. But if you're paying for coaching and getting a lecture, you're being cheated.

WHAT DOES A REAL COACH LOOK LIKE?

First, they MIGHT be very humble, low key, and maybe they aren't even wealthy.

I have several coaches for different purposes and they all fill a critical role in my personal and professional development.

Let me tell you about Bob.

Bob is just a regular guy. He has a background in construction and is responsible for facilities management for a major Chicago church.

Bob is very unassuming, puts on no airs, and is most comfortable in jeans and a baseball cap. I meet with Bob at least once a week and he has given me more insight into my business than any handbook, seminar, or guru ever has.

And you know what? Bob doesn't know the first thing about my business. He doesn't even understand what I do. What Bob does know is **human nature**, fundamental human nature and business **principles**, and most importantly ...

HE KNOWS HOW TO COACH!

Let's go back to the Tiger Woods example. Most people could not tell you the name of Tiger's coach. Why? He is not a famous golfer and will never be as good a player as Tiger. Tiger knows that he needs a coach who can EXAMINE his game and help him figure out where he's going wrong.

Tiger tried to go out on his own and failed ...BIG TIME! But his coach has kept him focused and playing brilliantly because while he can't drive the ball 320 yards down the middle of the fairway on a drizzly day like Tiger can, HE KNOWS HOW TO COACH effectively so Tiger can do it. Time after time. Round after round. The coach understands what makes Tiger purr, and that's the difference. Coaches aren't wannebes; coaching is its own skill set.

What about the superstar coaches - the ones we see on television and on magazine covers?

Let's talk some more about Michael Jordan. Once again you have the problem of a guy who has a very specific way of doing everything. Michael was very successful as a player, but no matter how hard ANYONE tries, NOBODY will be another Michael Jordan. Nobody should even try.

Even if it were possible to be another Michael Jordan, the WORST person to show you how to do it would be MICHAEL JORDAN.

Michael's talent lies in playing basketball, not coaching, not adult learning principles, but playing basketball.

SO, WHAT DOES A GOOD COACH LOOK LIKE ANYWAY?

There's no easy answer for that. The most important thing is that you need someone you can really connect with. For some people, I am the best coach in the world, but for others, I am the absolute worst. A coach must be able to spot your weaknesses and help you strengthen them. Conversely, a coach should be able to spot your strengths and guide you in capitalizing on them.

Let me give you some fundamental "must haves" to look for in a coach:

1. Your prospective coach should administer some kind of initial personal assessment. The first step in the growth process is self-awareness. I use several proprietary assessments to help clients clearly understand their thinking preferences and communication styles. This helps me immediately identify strengths and weaknesses. It also helps me target my coaching approach based on the results. At the VERY LEAST, your coach should administer an MBTI or similar assessment test.

2. You should have at least some access to your coach. Even if you are in a massively huge group coaching program, you need to be able to talk to SOMEONE. If you get value out of a large program, by all means, stick with it, BUT you need to find ANOTHER program to augment it where you can get feedback. Without direct feedback you are working in a vacuum. It's much like trying to bounce a ball against smoke. You need resistance to succeed.

3. Don't read too much into success stories and testimonials. At the end of the day, the only success story that counts is yours. I have been disappointed by many, many coaches, but then again, most don't know what they are doing. After having been trained and certified on FIVE different coaching systems, I can tell you that most people selling coaching programs don't have a clue what they are doing. I'm not saying that "certification" is everything. Plenty of certified

people are severely incompetent too. While some "uncertified" coaches are quite empathic and intuitive, I have found that this is the exception rather than the rule.

4. Most importantly, get a coach you like. You need to find someone you respect and enjoy interacting with. Remember not to base your respect COMPLETELY on that person's business experience, but also make sure the coach knows how to coach and has a genuine interest in your success, not just your checkbook.

Okay now once again, it's time to think about what you have learned for a few minutes... then take action. Just so you know, none if the advice in this book will work if you don't do those two things: follow instructions and take action! Just reading and absorbing won't get you to the finish line. So, are you ready?

Your 60 Second Strategy:

Get Smart

By

- Networking with colleagues to stay current about your corner of the world

- Striving to rarely be caught off guard by changes in the business environment

- Keeping up to date on what's happening around you (politically, socially, at home)

- Learning to synthesize new information and apply it to your goals and activities

- Determining your intelligence needs and where you will gather them

- Consuming all the knowledge you can about your target

- Gaining an in-depth understanding of your environment

- Learning how to "Connect the Dots" by anticipating future trends and recognizing patterns

- Learning to objectively assess your personal capabilities

- Establishing measurement systems to track your progress and serve as an early warning system

DO THIS NOW

1. Go to **www.60secondStrategist.com** and download the Get Smart worksheets.

2. Go to **www.SixtySigma.com** and download the worksheets on Selecting a Great Coach. Although Sixty Sigma Inc. only handles a very specific type of client, the website provides numerous free resources to anyone looking for a great coach.

3. Go back and look at your goals. Do you know everything you need to know to accomplish them? If not, make a separate list of what you need to know and where you can go to get that knowledge.

4. Start looking for new places you can go to expand your knowledge of your target. Perhaps a newsletter, book, or seminar will make you smarter on the subject.

5. Begin looking closely at the environment around you (that includes social, home, business, and all other components that apply to your life, such as church or synagogue) and your goals. Try to take a step back and gain a holistic view of your objectives and what the future holds for you.

6. Create a mind map of your goals. I highly recommend Tony Buzan's iMindMap software. It's more expensive than other products, but it's the best. Incidentally, Tony invented Mind Mapping, so you know he's the best! When you register for the FREE 60 Day Strategy Course at **www.60secondStrategist.com** you will receive a link for a FREE trial of the iMindMap software, plus several extra bonuses. Believe me, it's worth the click.

7. Based on your research and mind mapping, organize your data. Do you need to learn more? Do you need to put the brakes on the project or cancel it all together? Remember that recognizing problems in projects and killing them early is a very good thing. This allows you to focus on the worthwhile ones!

Chapter 4

"Analyze and Forecast"

"The power of intuitive understanding
will protect you from harm until
the end of your days."
-Lau Tzu

Keith Ferazzi is one of the most incredible speakers I have
ever had the pleasure of working with. Perhaps you know

him from his best-selling book, *Never Eat Alone*, or maybe you have seen him featured in the news as, "America's Best Networked Man."

Anyway... so we were doing a workshop for a bunch of marketing executives centered on the topic of innovation. Keith was happy to kick off the event with a big splash. I was actually hesitant to use Keith for this particular event because he is definitely not an innovation expert. Is that a problem for Keith? I think not.

The thing you need to realize is that innovation really has more to do with *thinking* and *taking* action that it does with computers, electronics, and gadgetry as many people assume.

Keith is a *thinker*.

We all showed up the morning of the workshop with the management of the client company. We set up a round table of executives where Keith was able to interview nine people at the same time to learn more about the company, current goals, challenges, and political climate. In less than half an hour, he was able to synthesize all the information and create a "story" to tell the company for his presentation.

The management and audience were very impressed with Keith's performance. Many felt he knew the company just as well as they did based on his ability to put the pieces together and really understand them.

Since then, I have worked extremely hard to develop this ability to better serve the companies I speak to and do workshops for. I must say, I think I'm pretty good at it now... but I really owe it all to Keith.

Does Keith have a lock on the thinking market? Absolutely not!

Let me tell you about a workshop I did where we got a whole room full of executives to build a story, just like me and Keith.

The workshop involved a pretty sophisticated scenario planning "game" that we worked on for several months. We had PhD's, MBA's, and all kinds of alphabet soup credentials on the team. It was laborious, expensive, and time consuming, but in the end, it paid off.

Basically, here's what we did:

We conducted interviews with several managers to gain insight about their predictions about the future of the company as they saw it, the industry as whole, key competitors, and the legal environment. We then looked externally at factors such as Wall Street, the economy, and potential changes in the political landscape.

For example, we might predict for the *industry*, "The industry will grow at a rate of 15-20% over the next 3-5 years." We then developed 5-10 possible alternate "futures" for the *industry* category. We might say, "Three major competitors will consolidate and overall growth will be flat for the next 3-5 years." We then wrote down each of these industry scenarios on green index cards.

Then, we created 5-10 scenarios for each of the other categories (e.g. political landscape, the economy, the company, etc). We put the political scenarios on red cards, the economic scenarios on blue cards, etc.

I won't get into the specifics here of how the "game" was played in the workshop (because much of the information is confidential and proprietary), but if you hire me, I'll be more than happy to sit down and create a game for your team!

We gathered the managers and divided them into teams of about five people per team. Each team was then tasked with building a "story of the future" by choosing a red card, a green card, a blue card, etc, and fitting those cards together to weave a story about how they would manage their business if the created story were to actually happen.

The results were nothing less than amazing! These guys, who thought they already knew everything, were able to see things from a fresh perspective for the first time in years!

Some groups became engaged in heated debates while others began calling back to the office to book meetings in order to implement some of the ideas they had come up with. The energy in the room crackled like static electricity and was nothing short of remarkable.

Toward the end of the day, one of the executives pulled me aside and asked me, "When are we going to get a copy of the report?"

Puzzled, I asked, "What report?"

He asked, "Aren't you going to summarize all the scenario planning we created in the room today? This stuff is golden! I need to share this stuff with my team. We are working on our business plans and need this stuff."

I told him, "This was just an exercise... a game if you will. The idea was just to get you guys to think."

"We haven't thought this well in years!" he exclaimed.

Shortly after, a panic spread throughout the room as managers realized that nobody from the staff was recording the "game" that was occurring at each table. In a mad rush, we had the staff begin collecting everyone's scratch paper, then taking notes to be summarized and distributed.

As it turned out, our little "game" that only lasted a few hours was used to help build multi-million dollar business plans. One huge campaign got its start in that small room on that cold winter day.

I can't help but think about another campaign that started in a small, empty room...

Before I go any further though, I'm going to warn you... I'm going to commit a big faux pas here and use a dirty word: politics. I know I have the potential to lose half of my audience here, but that's just a risk I'll have to take. Please stick with me.

I'll try not to offend anyone who is firmly in one armed camp or the other, but when it comes to business, you must look clearly at the political landscape and how whichever party is in power might affect your business plans. Believe me, it does matter.

I guess if you are so close minded that you can't learn from someone who isn't totally aligned with you politically... well... I guess that's your problem, not mine.

Anyway, here's the story.

I became friends with Andrea Seastrand when I was in fourth grade. Both me and my sister were involved in 4-H which gave us the opportunity to become involved in local government. I developed a strong desire to become more involved in community service and volunteered at my local State Assemblyman's office.

Assemblyman Eric Seastrand was one of the kindest, gentlest men I had ever met... and yes, he was a Republican (did I lose anyone yet?)

So Eric took me under his wing and taught me so much about serving my country, the legislative process, and caring for others. He was one of the rare public servants who considered himself just that - a public servant, unlike many self-serving politicians we read about today. From both parties. As a ten year old, I didn't quite understand the whole Republican-Democrat rivalry thing... I just knew that he was a loving, intelligent father figure to me... something I really needed in my life.

As I grew older, Eric introduced me to so many people... Governor Deukmejian, Speaker Willie Brown, and others. He even once took me out to lunch with Rush Limbaugh

(Rush wasn't as famous back then and didn't take himself so seriously). Eric managed to get me a personally autographed picture of Ronald Reagan with a *personalized* attached letter, which I still treasure.

Sadly, friends, family, constituents, and loved ones had to stand by hopelessly as Eric valiantly fought a losing battle with cancer. Eric passionately served his constituents and the State of California until the day he died.

Eric's wife, Andrea, bravely picked up the torch where he had dropped it and ran for his seat in the State Assembly. I worked closely with Andrea for several years, both as an Intern and a volunteer on her political campaigns. Just like Eric, Andrea showed me a loving kindness I have rarely seen from anyone else. Oh yeah... and she introduced me to a bunch of big shots... like Bob Dole and Sony Bono.

In 1994, Andrea ran against Walter Capps for an open US Congress seat in one of the most heated campaigns being waged that year across the country.

Andrea was labeled as a conservative by the media, and was targeted for defeat by a coalition of labor unions. The Capps campaign greatly benefitted from an 18-month labor union campaign to defeat Seastrand. The labor unions spent an estimated 3.2 million dollars in a mudslinging media blitz against Seastrand, an amount that exceeded the war chests of the Capps and Seastrand campaigns COMBINED.

Despite this, we were victorious and sent my good friend Andrea to Washington!

Victory can be quite fleeting in politics, as in life. Walter Capps ran against Andrea, once again in 1996. While driving home from a campaign event during the summer of 1996, Capps' vehicle was struck by a drunk driver- who, ironically, was one of his supporters. Capps was seriously injured and was unable to actively campaign during the summer months. However, the sympathy generated by the accident, the strong national Democratic tide in 1996, and the massive flow of labor union soft money combined to propel Capps to victory.

But the story doesn't end there... Capps' political victory was even shorter lived than Andrea's... Literally.

As a result of the car accident and what was rumored to be many years of self-medicating, Capps' physical and mental health spiraled downward. Capps died of a heart attack at Dulles Airport in Washington D.C. He was only nine months into his term. Several powerful people attended his funeral, including the Reverend Jesse Jackson.

Shortly after that... I got the call...

Andrea Seastrand was done with politics. She moved on to a non-partisan role as the Executive Director of the California Space and Technology Alliance. A wonderful move for a wonderful woman... Tom Bordonaro, who filled her old State Assembly position, decided to run for the open seat. It was now December, 1997.

I hurriedly flew from my home in Georgia to Santa Barbara, California to help run what turned out to be one of the most famous special congressional elections in the history of the state.

A special election was called and three major candidates stepped up to the plate. They were Walter's wife, Lois, Assemblyman Tom Bordonaro, and Brooks Firestone, a wealthy winemaker and heir to the Firestone Tire fortune.

I had less than a month to help out because I had other contractual commitments overseas, but I wanted to help as much as I could. The way the California special elections process works is a little odd. It's run like a regular primary election, with separate Republican and Democrat ballots, **BUT**... if any candidate secures 50% + 1 vote, that candidate wins and the election is over.

Our campaign had two primary sectors of focus. One was in Santa Barbara County and the other one was in San Luis Obispo County – this covered the entire Congressional District.

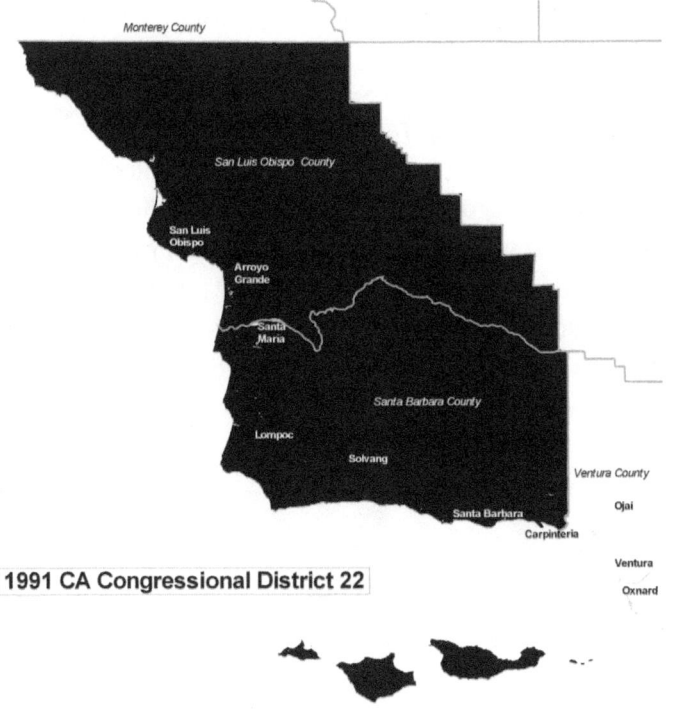

1991 CA Congressional District 22

I was tasked with managing the Santa Barbara County effort with the help of only a handful of people. When trying to cover such a large, heavily populated area, no matter how good the few people are, sometimes quantity is better than quality. I mean, do 100 really good votes count more than 100 mediocre votes?

We were seriously outspent by both opponents. Capps had millions from the labor unions and Firestone... well, DUH! Just look at the guy's last name. To make matters more difficult, Firestone was running as a Republican, effectively dividing the Republican vote amongst two candidates.

My goal was simple: to make sure that no other candidate won a simple majority. This would throw the race into a subsequent run-off election and allow the campaign a lot more time to get its ducks in a row.

We needed more time!

The good part (for me) was that I was put up in an enormous Santa Barbara mansion which overlooked the city. It was quite breathtaking! It was nice that a wealthy contributor let me "house sit" while they were on vacation. It would have been even nicer if I got paid to help out with the campaign! I guess if I wanted money, I should have worked for one of the other (and much better funded) candidates. Actually, I wanted to just hang out at this palace all day and play king of the hill, but I had work to do. Help win an election ... or in this case, make sure we at least didn't lose this round and would be able to fight another day.

Since my candidate currently represented San Luis Obispo at the state government level, he had very low name recognition in Santa Barbara. The main effort was in San Luis Obispo ...my job was just to minimize damage in the southern portion of the district. Since Walter Capps was from Santa Barbara previously, his wife had very high name recognition, plus the aforementioned press, which made our job extremely difficult.

So, there I was on day one ...just me, two other people, and a room full of telephones. Did I mention I hate talking on the phone? Those telephone cords might as well have been coiled snakes. I wasn't about to reach out and touch one of them.

My phone-aphobia began in college; I sold business communication solutions (phone systems) for MCI over the - wait for it ..... phone. Granted, I made a lot of money doing it, but I still hated every minute of it. Still do. To this day, I avoid the phone whenever I can.

Anyway, there I was with nothing but a room full of phones and two people staring at me wondering what we were going to do. Then it hit me! I needed to mobilize more people to do the legwork for me. I don't think I was being particularly clever, I just didn't want to talk on the phone. If my strategy had been to start calling voters, the other two people in the room would have gotten pretty angry if I just sat there reading Newsweek while they worked.

Have you ever voted in a special election? If you are like most people, you have not. So, here's the deal: most people know that our elected officials have a hard enough time getting people out to vote during a general election. This is when they are voting for multiple offices, propositions, and issues. Things they actually care about.

Do you know how hard it is to get people out to vote when it's just for one race?

The only people who typically vote in these cases are those who are extremely passionate about politics. The *normal* people stay home and watch TV.

So, who cared enough about this election to go out and vote?

The special interest groups did, that's who!

You know … groups like the NRA, PETA, NOW, Right-to-Life, Churches, Synagogues, and ACLU types. Each and every group has a core of rabid supporters who are ready to do battle for their cause.

The trick was to get more of our special interest group members out to vote than our opponents could. In this election, it really didn't matter what average people thought because wild horses couldn't drag them to the polling place. They just didn't care enough to show up. The focus needed to be on those hard core voters who did care.

So, all we did was figure out which special interest groups were on our side, aroused their passion for this important election, then got them to contact their members on our behalf. Think about it …who are you going to listen to anyway? Some dude you don't know who calls you on the phone … or your chapter president of the *Surfers Alliance*?

After just a couple days spent making targeted phone calls (yes, I sucked it up and made them) and meeting with a few influential community leaders face to face, my work was done. By the end of the first week, hundreds of volunteers were calling their friends, putting out flyers, and canvassing door-to door. And it was all not so much in an effort to help my candidate; it was in support of their particular issue. People are generally self-serving, which is good to remember when you're pushing a product, an agenda, or a candidate. Identify the self-interest and you're half way home.

It was beautiful! A true grass-roots effort. I didn't want to get really involved anyway. I mean, who was I to tell people how to vote? I just found the people that were already passionate about their issues and gave them a little nudge in the right direction.

Okay, so now I guess I have to tell you the end result of all this.

Were we successful?

Here is the January 14th (1998) headline from the Los Angeles Times:

WIDOW LEADS IN SPECIAL ELECTION FOR REP. CAPPS' SEAT

Quotes from the article include:

"Tens of thousands of absentee ballots were cast before the polls even opened, suggesting that turnout could exceed 50%, an unusually high rate of participation for a preseason election."

And ...

"With roughly one-third of precincts reporting, Capps led a six-candidate field with 49% of the vote—easily enough to finish first, but just barely short of the 50% needed to win election outright."

Bordonaro was also quoted as saying, "There doesn't seem to be any real burning issues, or central focus for people to rally around," noting (and echoing my previous statement) that residents seemed to care more about individual concerns.

The turnout for Santa Barbara for my candidate blew away all expectations. My goal had been to quickly rally enough votes to hold off the opponent and force a runoff election.

MISSION ACCOMPLISHED!

I got on a plane and flew to South Korea with a big smile on my face! My candidate was given a second chance ... to prove to the voters he was worthy. Unfortunately, my services were not available during the next election. Tom was unsuccessful in securing the seat. Were those two facts connected? Who knows?

Perhaps things would have been different if I had been there to help. I like to think I could have made a difference, but that ship sailed without me, and ended up running aground. Tom is a very resilient man who, like my wife, serves others from the confines of a wheelchair.

He continues to faithfully serve the community as the San Luis Obispo County Assessor.

Lois Capps has managed to keep her congressional seat secure by benefitting from one of the most unscrupulous congressional district gerrymandering in the history of the United States.

For those of you who don't know... this is where they re-draw the district boundaries to ensure ongoing political victory for the incumbent. The 23rd Congressional District is now known as the "Ribbon of Shame".

The new district follows the coastline for nearly 200 miles from Monterey County, all the way into Ventura County. The contorted district is no more than five miles wide in most places and as narrow as 100 Yards wide in some places as it tightly follows the coast in search of Democratic voters and avoiding Republican households.

Go back and compare this to the original district map. Is something fishy going on here?

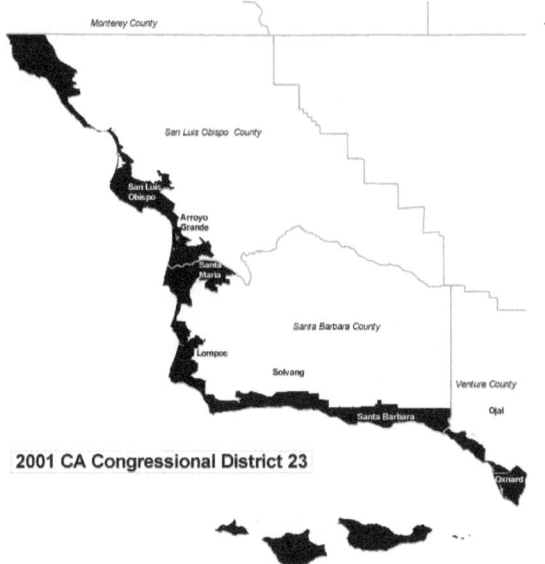

2001 CA Congressional District 23

This redistricting has been deemed so unethical that is has fueled a nationwide movement of political reform for the creation of 'fairly' drawn political districts that do not favor one political party over another.

But hey, I'm not really into politics anymore. And I'm sure it goes on in every state and in both parties. I just find this type of shenanigans really interesting.

So, if you're still with me and you haven't dropped out to go and protest your government . . .

Your 60 Second Strategy:

Analyze & Forecast

By

- Learning to spot problems before they occur

- Seeking out and finding new opportunities **before** others find them

- Visualizing how multiple scenarios will play out in the future

- Developing the skill of predicting the results of your actions and the actions of others

- Knowing and understanding the forces (political, international, climate, market, social) that will impact your strategy

- Conducting an internal and an external SWOT analysis of your journey

- Considering your risk exposure for each venture you undertake

- Visualizing the best and worst case outcome scenarios of your plan

- Building a "story" about how your plan will play out

- Openly broadcasting your plans and intentions to colleagues and friends

DO THIS NOW

1. Go to **www.60secondStrategist.com** and download the *Analyze Forces* worksheets.

2. Using the worksheets, complete an **internal** SWOT analysis of your objectives.

3. Now, complete the **external** SWOT Analysis worksheet.

4. Put the two side by side. Does anything stand out? Look for consistencies, inconsistencies and red flags.

5. Tell a story of the present based on what you see happening in the worksheets. Say it out loud. Does it make sense? (You are in your private 'don't bother me' space right?)

6. Create a "worst case scenario" story of the future based on the worksheets and your analysis.

7. Create a "best case" scenario.

8. Now, get creative… create at least one alternate scenario and one "crazy" improbable, but not impossible, scenario.

9. Decide whether or not to proceed with the pursuit of your objective. If it's still a go, begin to specifically detail what success looks like. Write a story about your successful outcome and share it with others.

Chapter 5

"Set Your Plan"

"If you have accomplished all that you
have planned for yourself,
you have not planned enough."
-Edward Everett Hale

Have you ever been to a big trade show? I mean a BIG
one? These things rock! For a few years, I had the pleasure
of travelling around the country and setting up multi-

million dollar campaigns for national conventions. One part of me said, "Hey, this whole thing is a waste of money," while another side said, "This stuff is really cool!"

I must say that this is where I have seen the best creativity in action. Companies will do anything to attract visitors to their booth. It started originally with give-away pens... then books, then leather journals. Finally, many associations began placing dollar limits on the "prizes" we gave away. Then it was a new contest to see who could give away the coolest stuff that costs less than $20 per visitor.

We stared serving fresh cappuccino and crepes, but that was soon outdone by the booth offering free massages. Then, one of my partners came up with a virtual reality booth that simulated what it's like to ride a bus with paranoid schizophrenia. The competitors answered with a booth where a volunteer sits in a dentist chair with electrodes attached to her brain. A computer analyzed her thoughts and drew a multicolored painting in real time in front of an audience. Imagine seeing a picture of raw fear!

One of my friends from another company was pretty upset because we were only allowed to give away pens and books at a particular show. They managed to "beat the system" in a way. They gave away a $20 book written by Lorraine Bracco (Dr. Melfi from HBO's The Soprano's). Instead of just giving the book away, they had Lorraine Bracco sit in the booth and sign everyone's book. The mob couldn't have kept people away! I mean if Tony Soprano was crazy about her . . .

Okay, so I had a point here somewhere... Putting up an 80'x120' exhibit that is 20' tall with engravers, plasma

TV's and cappuccino bars is no small undertaking. It takes several people over several days to make sure everything is in place. In the end, nobody cares what snags happened or how I overcame problems... they just needed to get the job done.

I would usually show up three days or so before opening day, to make sure we got everything set up without any problems. Well, in one particular case, the association was really ticked off at us because my marketing team decided to cut our booth space in half, just a few months before the convention.

Unfortunately, you can't just "pull out" and take a small space when you reserved a big space. First, you have to pay a deposit of several hundreds of thousands up front. Then, the exhibit people draw out a floor plan based on how much space people buy. They put together a very detailed map with hundreds of exhibitors, lounges, eating areas, etc. Due to safety regulations, the exhibit manager has to submit the plan to the fire marshal for approval, usually several months in advance. When you wait till the last minute to pull out, you inconvenience literally thousands of people and cost everyone tons of money.

Needless to say, the exhibit folks were ticked off when we said we wanted the smaller space. We didn't care that we would still be on the hook for the big booth space. We just didn't want to pay the million dollars + it would cost to actually build a booth to fit into such a large footprint.

After many arguments, the association finally agreed, but moved our booth from the very front of the hall... to... you guessed it... to the very back of the hall... right by the loading docks and in the closest possible proximity to the trash dumpsters. Not only was this bad from an exhibiting standpoint, it was bad from a setup standpoint. Our booth and materials arrived in large crates, as always, but we couldn't verify the contents.

Why? Because our booth was placed in the middle of the "highway" of forklifts that delivered all the crates to all of the other booths. We weren't even allowed to open our crates until the end of the first day. It gets even more complicated because we had a union agreement to employ so many people and we couldn't just send them home because we couldn't fully utilize them yet. We couldn't have them work all night after the traffic cleared either.

So what did we do? Me, my foreman "Speedy," and a team of executive consultants, took off our cufflinks, rolled up our sleeves, and spent the night opening crates and organizing everything.

It wasn't until the next day that we realized that we were missing a giant billboard panel for the booth. We were due to have the grand opening the next day and we had a 4'x6' giant hole in the wall of our booth where a backlit sign was supposed to be.

Did I mention that is was Saturday... we were in San Francisco and our warehouse was in Chicago?

Immediately, I called a team meeting... not just my team, but with all my friends on the convention floor. We had electricians, carpenters, AV guys, booth managers. I gave them the following speech:

"Okay, guys, thanks for stopping by our booth... we got
a real problem. We are missing one of our large booth
panels. It wasn't in the crate. Now we have a hole in our
booth. A bunch of VP's and General Managers from the
company are coming by in a few hours and they don't
have a clue that anything is wrong. I am taking them all
out to eat at the Ritz-Carlton tonight, so we need to get
started on a plan right now... because I'll be out of the
loop for a few hours. We usually have our backup panels
with nothing more than the company logo, but those
were missing in the shipment too, so at this time, we have
absolutely nothing to put in the gaping huge main wall of
the booth. This can't be a cheap duct-tape solution. We
have millions invested here and there will be some pretty
angry people if the booth doesn't look right."

What ensued was a highly energized brainstorming session
with some of the finest minds in the tradeshow business.
We finally came up with the following solutions:

1. We had someone compile a list of all the shows on the
    west coast where we have properties. We then tried
    to locate a rush courier to get us one of our generic
    panels by morning.

2. There is only one company in the country with the
    ability to rush produce a copy of the missing panel.
    Fortunately for us, that company had a facility in San
    Francisco. Unfortunately for us, there were other
    people with similar emergencies in San Francisco, so
    we were at the back of the line... In fact; we weren't
    even in the line. I had one of my graphic guys start
    working his political connections to get us at the front
    of the line.

3. Even if we got to the front of the line to get the panel printed, we didn't have the CD-ROM with the art files with us. Our creative agency was in New Jersey and nobody was at the office (remember... it was Saturday). Finally, we got in touch with one of the project managers who lived in Manhattan. We made her cancel her hot date and sent her back to the office to get the art files.

4. Meanwhile, I had one of my technology buddies set up a secure FTP site where our agency project manager could upload the art files and the printer in San Francisco could download them and make our panel. We knew we were cutting it REALLY close because these panels take several hours to actually print.

5. For our third backup, we secured an additional large plasma TV. We already had one TV in the booth running a pre-recorded demonstration loop. It was easy enough to add another TV to the loop, but...

6. The free-standing wall where the panel was missing was not created to support an additional large TV. Plus, the TV was still much smaller than the hole in the wall. We gathered a team of carpenters to re-build the wall to support a TV and install mounting hardware for it. Also, they needed to finish the wall so it blended with the booth.

Whew!

After assignments were delegated, I put my exhibit foreman in charge. My team of consultants followed me back to our hotel to get changed and enjoy a nice dinner at the Ritz-Carlton with the management team. We had to sip wine, tell jokes, back slap, and act like everything was under control.

I grew nervous as the night grew later and my phone didn't ring. One franchise General Manager put his hand on my shoulder and asked, "So, how's the booth looking?"

I nervously responded, "We are just putting on the finishing touches... we'll be done by morning."

He said, "I have only seen the booth in concept drawings. What do you say we stop by the convention center after dinner and check it out?"

I told him, "Nah... I don't think that'll be necessary. Besides, set up hours officially close at ten and it's almost ten-thirty now. They probably won't let us in. Why don't you just stop by early tomorrow before the booth opens and I'll give you the grand tour."

He smiled and said, "That'll be just fine."

Rhoda, one of the consultants, overheard the conversation and noticed my nervousness. She told me, "Relax, you left Speedy in charge. If there was a problem, he would have called. You really have to learn to trust the plan and trust your people."

"Okay, Rhoda," I said. "I'll trust Speedy. He knows the plan and he knows what to do. He has been running booths for over 20 years. I'll trust him and let go."

At around midnight, my mobile phone rang. It was Speedy. He said, "We got it all taken care of. No need to get into the details, but it's done. We're all pretty tired now and we're going to go bed. I'll walk you through everything first thing in the morning. Will that be okay?"

"Sure, Speedy," I agreed. "We'll see you tomorrow."

The next morning, I entered the booth to find a new plasma TV seamlessly embedded into the newly rebuilt booth wall. It was beautiful! I congratulated Speedy, patted him on the back and asked him why he went with this option instead of the others.

Speedy informed me, "Well, the people in New Jersey got the art disc, but we were never able to pull enough strings to get to the front of the printing line. They only have one machine and it was busy all night. We might be able to get in line today, but that's too late. We called everywhere to try and find someone to get one of the backup panels. Either the panels were locked in 'inaccessible' storage or we couldn't find a courier. Really, our only option was to have our team of carpenters, decorators, and electricians rebuild the wall and embed the TV in it. I'm sure glad we keep the blueprints with us. Once we got working, it really wasn't a big deal at all."

Shortly after, the product management team from the company came by the booth. They were completely impressed with everything. Even though many of them were present in several of the design meetings, not a single person even noticed that we had modified the booth.

Planning and teamwork can save you from disaster, but let me warn you... it's not a guarantee of success. Sometimes you can do everything right and things can go wrong... very wrong.

The hardest battles you can ever face are the ones you aren't expecting and the ones where you are an unwilling participant. You are often unarmed and ill prepared.

I must admit that both of these facts were true when my first marriage ended. I won't go into details, but I was blindsided and completely unprepared for this dramatic change in my life. I allowed it to affect my career, finances, and other personal relationships.

A second marriage to my beautiful, intelligent, loving wife, Leslie, provided me and my family with a wonderful fresh start. While still recovering from devastating financial setbacks related to the divorce, we found true happiness that no amount of money could buy.

The real measure of your wealth is how much you'd be worth if you lost all your money.
~Author Unknown

So there we were, the five of us... me, Leslie and our three kids, living in a tiny two-story, three bedroom house... about 1,000 square feet. Trust me, it was really small. Those three bedrooms were the size of walk-in closets, only not as spacious.

As I mentioned earlier, Leslie is paralyzed from the waist down from a car accident. This house had very narrow hallways and doorways which made it very difficult for her to get around. Making things even more difficult, it was two stories, with the bedrooms upstairs. I carried Leslie up the stairs to go to bed at night and down the stairs before I left for work in the morning. If she forgot something upstairs after I went to work … too bad.

Leslie couldn't even get her wheelchair into the tiny downstairs powder room, so I had to rip the door off the hinges so she could get through the doorway. She had no privacy, but at least she wasn't miserable all day.

We knew we would eventually need a bigger house, but were trying to recover financially before we made any new investments or took on new debt. We also didn't want to install an expensive stair lift in the house because we knew we would be moving relatively soon.

I was in a developmental position at work and anxiously waiting for a big (expected) promotion. It was rare that anyone in that department stayed longer than 12-18 months without getting promoted… and I mean nobody. Since my accomplishments and credentials were MUCH greater than my peers, I knew it was just a matter of time before I got my big break. After I passed my 1-year anniversary in the department, I knew it would be just a matter of days before I got promoted.

But… being the pragmatic planner that I am, I did not want to count my chickens before they hatched. Leslie and I decided to wait for my promotion before looking to buy a new house.

But wait, there's more…

To further complicate things... the kids were going through a really bad, rebellious spell. My twin son and daughter from my first ill-fated marriage, Josh and Jordan, were going through their terrible two's... BIG TIME!

Carter, from Leslie's first marriage, was also two... and yes, folks, he was going through the terrible two's as well. It was the trifecta of tantrums in our household. Throw in the jealousy angle that's always at play with siblings trying to gain attention from Mommy and Daddy, and you have one big fit-throwing toy-strewn mess.

Picture a 115 pound petite young woman trying to chase down three rebellious two-year-olds in a wheelchair, navigating the narrow corridors of a tiny house. Not a fun task. I thought my job was stressful. I have always admired Leslie so much for being able to manage the house from a wheelchair while I was safely at work.

Finally, the kids got to be too much... Leslie needed help, so we decided to get an au pair. For those of you who don't know, an au pair is different than a nanny. These are young girls (usually) that come from another country to work as a child-care helper for a year. It's kinda like a foreign exchange student, but they only have to take two college classes while they are here... and they spend the rest of their time helping out with the kids... and partying when you aren't watching.

So we found our au pair and waited for her to come from El Salvador. We really couldn't afford it, but we REALLY needed the help. Plus, we knew that we couldn't afford to have one of the kids injured by climbing up on something where Leslie couldn't reach them. Boys will be boisterous, right? Besides, I was just days from my promotion. We knew that we needed to solve the house problem quickly because, by law, the au pair needed to have her own room.

So now, all three two-year-olds were living in a tiny 8x10 room. There wasn't even enough room for beds! We had to get a trundle bed that we tucked away during the day as well as a tiny toddler bed. That was the only way we could fit all three kids in the room. The other day, I asked Leslie what she remembered about the setup in that room. She reminded me that she didn't know because she couldn't get her wheelchair in there. It was too small.

Just when I thought things couldn't get more complicated, they did.

One day Leslie called me at work and invited me to go out to lunch with her. I agreed and met her and Carter at one of our favorite Mexican restaurants (the twins were with their mother that day).

I was expecting a nice romantic lunch, but Leslie's mood was quite apprehensive. She was obviously nervous and holding something back, but wasn't letting me in on what it was. Things were getting so stressful with the house and the kids... I had been working 85+ hours a week at work.... I really couldn't handle much more. Neither could she.

Finally, she broke down crying and said, "I'm pregnant!"

I was dumbfounded! I really didn't know what to say. We had talked about having a baby together... someday, but that was not today. We had agreed not to talk about it until we were more financially secure and the kids we already had were older. To add to my confusion was the fact that my doctor had told me that I couldn't have kids! My twins were the result of in-vitro fertilization due to my low sperm count.

So, now, Leslie was pregnant with our "Miracle Baby." Sometimes I wish I could be in charge of when miracles happen, because the timing of this one really sucked.

So now, things got really complicated. On top of the other stuff, we had to figure out how SEVEN of us were going to live in a tiny three-bedroom house... and we couldn't make the au pair share a room. Putting the new baby in the kids' room was unthinkable - Leslie couldn't get in there, and a crying newborn would keep the other three awake.

Also, a big reason why Leslie was crying about the pregnancy was that her last pregnancy caused multiple health complications that she was not prepared to deal with. Here's the short list of what I had to watch my wife suffer through:

1. Due to her paralysis, Leslie suffers from muscle atrophy which has led to osteoporosis. This is a real bummer. She wasn't even 30 at the time and had to take osteoporosis medication. Her low bone density had already led to a broken ankle. If they ever invent a cure for paralysis (which I pray for every day), Leslie may still be stuck in a wheelchair if her bones continue to deteriorate. Leslie's first pregnancy significantly sped up the progression of her osteoporosis. The baby growing inside her just sucked the calcium right out of her bones. Leslie was now forced to discontinue her osteoporosis medication, thus furthering the

progression of the disease and increasing her health risk.

2. After Leslie's first pregnancy, she had developed neurogenic bladder, a common problem with paralyzed people. For those of you who don't know, most paralyzed people can't go to the bathroom like everyone else does. They have no bladder control. In Leslie's case, she has to use a catheter every 3-4 hours. You know how sometimes you can't find a bathroom and just have to hold it? Well, Leslie can't do that. If she misses her time window, she will just pee on herself. She has no bladder control. To make matters worse, Leslie's neurogenic bladder condition causes her bladder to have spasms with no warning, causing her to pee on herself. She finally got this under control with medication, but now was forced to stop that medication due to the pregnancy. Could it get even worse? You bet. You know how pregnant women have to pee all the time? Leslie had those issues too... except she can't tell when she has to "go". Leslie knew she would have to suffer the humiliation of wearing Depends adult diapers for the next nine months. Since our shower was upstairs and she had no way of getting to it, she had to smell like urine all day if she had an accident in the morning. Not really fun...

3. On top of everything else, Leslie suffered from terrible morning sickness for the ENTIRE pregnancy. This isn't your average morning sickness... we are talking about 'round the clock death-like symptoms. She would often vomit 10-12 times a day. She was dizzy, nauseous and exhausted... did I mention she had to chase around three wild two-year-olds all day? On top of that, due to

the house setup and her wheelchair, she wasn't always able to get to a nice trashcan or toilet to throw up in, which meant she would often throw up on herself or on the floor. Ever see a sick, pregnant, paralyzed woman in a wheelchair trying to bend over her bulging tummy trying to clean puke off the floor with three two-year-olds running around the house like wild animals? I haven't either, but I would have to hear the horror stories as I comforted Leslie after a hard day at work. I worked from home when I could and got friends and family to help out, (while we were still waiting for the au pair to arrive), but there were some days that   Leslie had to be alone, for which I still feel terrible guilt. The doctors gave her the strongest anti-nausea medication they could prescribe (the hard-core stuff they give to chemotherapy patients), but that wasn't even powerful enough.

4. I almost forgot about the edema. Most people know that pregnant women often suffer from edema and their feet can get really swollen. Many paralyzed people have severe edema problems without being pregnant. When you combine the two... you are talking serious problems. Shoes were a constant problem for Leslie. They would constantly give her pressure sores. Even the best orthopedic shoes caused problems because, due to her paralysis, she suffers from a condition called "hammer toe" (I swear I'm not making this up), where her toes involuntarily curl under her feet when she puts shoes on. The circulation is then cut off to her toes causing pressure sores. In an effort to alleviate the situation, Leslie quit wearing shoes around the house to "air out" her feet. Our hallways and doorways in the house were so narrow that Leslie

would constantly scrape up her toes on doorways. The combination of the edema, buckle toe, pressure sores, and scrapes led to the nastiest foot abscesses you ever saw. Due to Leslie's pregnancy, they could only use certain antibiotics which she was on for several months with little success. In the end, they had to cut off the end of her big toe to stop the infection from spreading.

In addition to Leslie's medical problems, our housing situation became even more drastic. We knew we had to move into a bigger house for sure, but I was still waiting on the big promotion. If we installed a stair lift in our current house, it would make it much less desirable in the housing market. Plus... those things can be pretty expensive. As Leslie's pregnancy progressed, I became increasingly nervous about carrying her up and down our steep staircase every day. She never got too heavy during the pregnancy... I don't even know if she passed 150 pounds, but I knew that one stumble could seriously hurt Leslie and endanger the baby's life.

We took a bold move and bought a bigger house. We saw no other option and just left the details to God.

Meanwhile, I focused a majority of my energy on my work... to get that much needed transfer and promotion to another department.

Now, here's the reason I'm sharing all this tragedy and turmoil with you, which is something I rarely do.

Over the previous several years, I had worked hard to build an extensive network of several hundreds of people throughout the company. Now it was time to start calling in some favors. Within several weeks, I found out about several opportunities throughout the company and was invited to several interviews. The reception of feedback was incredibly positive for EVERY SINGLE INTERVIEW. The strange thing is that I was extremely well qualified for these jobs… much better qualified than my competition, yet I wasn't getting any job offers. I kept plugging away, but was still curious why I was having trouble getting promoted for the first time in my career. I had weekly coaching conversations with my boss where he would advise me on interviewing tips and ways of improving my "brag book" portfolio, yet I still wasn't getting any offers.

After five or so rejections, I was sure I had found the job that was the perfect fit. I had an immediate connection with the hiring manager who wasn't much older than me. He went to University of Chicago School of Business, so we swapped some MBA war stories. I had actually worked with him on a few initiatives over the past several years. His wife was from El Salvador which made for interesting conversation because so was my au pair… oh, yeah and my mom was born there (although not El Salvadorian heritage).

To improve the situation even more, I was friends with *his* boss back from my convention days. I made friends with the boss during his first week with the company. He showed up at one of my big shows in New York City… I bought him a nice dinner at this place… What was it called… Rue 21? Rue 54?… wait, isn't that a store in the mall? I think Rue was in the name… anyway, I bought him a nice hunk of meat and a $120 Cognac, so we were friends for years.

I didn't want to rely completely on those relationships alone, so I dug deep into my network. I knew people in various parts of their marketing team, sales force (both managers and representatives), sales training staff, and legal compliance team. I was able to gain access to every critical document relating to this department. I analyzed and memorized their business plans, interviewed dozens of people and had many of them call the hiring manager to give enthusiastic recommendations on my behalf.

From my research, I was able to create an updated business plan for the department, a new sales force selling model, and even a software system to enhance the CRM capabilities of their sales force.

My job interview turned into a series of advisory meetings where I educated the management about crucial steps they needed to take as a department and as a brand. There was an apparent hold up in HR as far as the promotion was concerned, but I pretty much had the job. I wasn't concerned in the least.

Even though I didn't have the job, "in writing," Leslie and I decided to celebrate. We then felt a little more comfortable about buying the new house. She was starting to get bigger and didn't feel safe having me carry her up and down the steep staircase much longer. We ended up finding our "dream house" only a few blocks from our current house.

Our new house was about three times the size with room for everyone... even the au pair.

I waited impatiently to get word about the promotion... I got REALLY giddy when one of my best friends heard my boss say to a group of people, "...Oh yeah... he's got the job. He's definitely got the job." Incidentally, my boss used to work in that department and was friends with many of the managers there.

Then, I'll never forget that fateful Friday... A friend... who was also drinking buddies with the hiring manager's boss... approached me by the coffee machine with a sense of urgency. He said, "They just got clearance from HR to make you... or *someone* a job offer. They are going on a trip to New York today and need to make the decision before they leave."

I smiled and said, "That's great, so what's the problem?"

He pulled me away from the crowd at the coffee machine and whispered, "They love your work. They love what you have done for them already. A ton of people have called in to recommend you without even being asked."

Again I asked, "So, what's the problem?"

He pulled me even closer and whispered even softer, "What they want to know is... 'if this guy is so great, how come his boss hasn't called to recommend him?' The bottom line is, if your boss calls today, you got the job. If he doesn't call, you don't get the job."

I confidently said, "Well, that's no problem. My boss has been coaching me through this whole interview process. He already told me I am going to get "Exceeded Expectations" on my next performance review. In fact, I asked him what he would say if a manager wants to know what my biggest weakness is. My boss told me he would say, 'He has no weaknesses that impact his ability to do the job.'"

My buddy stepped back and said, "Well, that's good, but just make sure he makes the call this morning. These guys are getting on a plane right after lunch."

I ran straight into my boss's office. There were a few people hanging out in there and he said, "Hey, Tony, what's up? Any word on that job yet?"

I smiled and proclaimed, "Yes! I got the job! They are just waiting for you to call and give the thumbs up! Can you call 'em now so we can get things rolling?"

There was an awkward silence... then the office visitors began to excuse themselves from the room. My boss then motioned for me to close the door so we could talk.

He then said, "Why do they need me to call today? It doesn't all depend on me. There are lots of reasons who may or may not get the job. Who told you this anyway?"

I responded, "Someone from the management team told me this morning that the only thing stopping me from getting the job is you. If you call, I get the job. If you don't call, I don't get the job."

He leaned back in his chair, folded his arms and said with a smug look, "So, what exactly to you want me to tell them?"

I was flabbergasted. "What do you mean? You have been coaching me for weeks on the various personalities in the department and what they want and need to hear! Why don't you tell them what they need to hear? Tell them what you told me you would tell them! Remember all that stuff about, 'He has no real weaknesses... I plan to give him an *Exceeds Expectations* review.' What about that?"

After a long pause, he said, "No I'm not going to do that. I will tell them that you are an adequate worker... and that they should only hire you if they are totally desperate and have no other available candidates."

I was waiting for him to burst out laughing... or for someone to come out from behind the bookshelf saying, "You're on Candid Camera!"

No such luck.

Then it all hit me. He was the reason I didn't get the half dozen other jobs I had interviewed for. He's the reason these guys hesitated to hire me. He's the reason my fast-track career had come to a screeching halt.

Then it really, hit me... the promotion wasn't going to happen... not now...not ever. I was floating two mortgages. The housing market was dead and I didn't even have any nibbles on my old house.

Despite all of my hard work, performance history, and networking... this one guy, this one jerk... crushed every intricate plan I had created. The difficult part is that really... I should have seen it coming. For my whole career, my bosses loved me and appreciated my hard work and how I contributed to the organization. This guy didn't love me... and my intuition told me that, but I didn't want to see it and didn't accept it. Who paid the price for my ignorance? Me, not him....

Then I started to look to the future... Leslie and I had more money *going* out than *coming in*... not a problem short term, but this was not sustainable long term.

With this company, all it takes is one manager in your past to not like you and your entire career is dead. Everything I had worked for over the past seven years was destroyed. The beautiful crystal punch bowl that was my career was filled with delicious juice, but there was one piece of ugly brown detritus floating in the middle that was spoiling everything. How had I missed that?

I forgot about being a hard core infantry officer and all around tough guy... Everything was now piling up on me... my wife's poor health... the 87 hour work weeks... my own declining health... the rowdy kids... the financial setbacks... and now, my beacon of light... that promotion... was just killed. Now and forever... I was too devastated to even look for the lesson.

I will admit, I broke down crying... right there in his office. I couldn't hold it in anymore.

Through my sobbing and tears, I finally managed to say, "Why? Why are you doing this to me?"

He gave me a smug smile and said, "Come on. You knew. You knew I didn't like you."

I kept crying… "I have asked you for performance feedback every week for the past year and you have never said anything negative about my work. Every performance review you have given me has been stellar. The 360° feedback report you just completed for me was exceptional. How was I supposed to know anything?"

"You knew. You knew." He repeated the phrase but offered no other explanation for his hatred.

"So is this going to go on forever? Are you going to do this to me for every job I apply for? How can I make things right with you?"

"I dunno… I haven't decided yet."

"Do you realize I have a pregnant wife in a wheelchair and three kids to support?"

"That's not my problem!"

I calmly replied, "I know it's not. I just don't understand. Why are you doing this to me? What did I do wrong? If you had a problem with me or my performance, why didn't you tell me?"

"You knew. You knew."

Needless to say, I did not get the job. When the hiring manager called me to deliver the bad news, the reason given was simple, "Lack of total management support." But was that the end of me?

No.

Is that the end of my story?

No way!

Part of mastering strategy is learning from every experience and every mistake and applying it to create a better future. Often it takes some time and distance, as it did for me, to be able to put losses and setbacks into perspective, but eventually you can. You learn from them and you move on.

I misread my boss. I failed to heed my own instincts about our relationship. I allowed someone else to hold my career hostage. I removed the brown detritus from the punch bowl.

I tell this story to illustrate two main points:

1. Sometimes, no matter how well you plan and execute, you will lose. You are not omniscient and you can't control everything and everybody.

2. You must accept failure and opposition as a critical part of success.

I am reminded of this fact by Diane L. Coutu, senior editor at Harvard Business Review who teaches us:

"MORE THAN EDUCATION, more than experience, more than training, a person's level of resilience will determine who succeeds and who fails. That's true in the cancer ward, it's true in the Olympics, and it's true in the boardroom."

Your 60 Second Strategy:

Set Your Plan

By

- First, before you launch your plan, deciding on the right tools to get the job done

- Clearly identifying the "Who, What, Where, and When" in your project planning

- Being creative in your project planning

- Seeking to understand how your actions will impact others

- Mapping out your entire plan from beginning to end

- Clearly identifying exactly what you will need to get the job done

- Telling everyone involved what their job is and what you need them to do

- Anticipating snags and problems before they arise

- Having back up plans ready to go, just in case something goes wrong (it will!)

- Building a strong team of friends and allies

DO THIS NOW

1. Go to www.60secondStrategist.com and download the Set your Plan worksheets.

2. Develop a POA (Plan of Action) using the worksheets provided or other project management tools such as iMindMap, Excel, MS Project, or a good ol' fashioned piece of paper.

3. Make a list of major obstacles (or people) that can interfere with your plan or kill it entirely.

4. Develop contingency plans in anticipation of the most likely negative events.

5. Make a list of everyone and everything you need to make your plan succeed.

6. Get yourself motivated, pumped up and excited! Start telling everyone you know! It's almost time to kick things into action! (But if you have a boss like I did, don't tell him.)

Chapter 6

"Get It Done!"

"When you do nothing, you feel overwhelmed and powerless. But when you get involved, you feel the sense of hope and accomplishment that comes from knowing you are working to make things better."
-Pauline R. Kezer"

I felt the warm blood gushing from my temple and running down my cold cheek as I crawled like a worm... no... more like a Halibut through the rocky trench. I strained my neck to lift my head from the mud. The laceration, previously numbed by the frigid night air, became increasingly painful each time I dragged my face across the rough earth.

"Get your ******* head down," was the only warning Jock gave as he pressed the hard heel of his boot into my cheek, driving my face deeper in the mud.

"Airborne! Just do what he says! We are almost done for tonight."

"How do you know, *Tiny*?" I gasped as I struggled to squirm out from under Jock's boot.

"I see light over the horizon... morning is almost here. They have to stop..."

"Shut up! Shut Up! Shut the **** up!" *Jock* screamed out of frustration. "Did I give you weasels permission to speak? Just for that... you all need to turn around and go across the field again."

I heard a whimper emanating from the mud 10 feet behind me, but dared not respond.

Jock removed his combat boot from my face and headed off toward the pathetic voice. I strained to hear the conversation, but my mud-filled ears heard nothing but mumbling.

"Mercy, you want mercy? I have already given you too much mercy! I am already way too lenient with you stupid weaklings! I don't care if the field is 100 yards long. We'll cross it ten times if we have to... oh, and yes, we have time. We have plenty of time. Your *brother*, *Tiny*, doesn't have a watch, but I do. It's only 0300 hours..."

That exchange was so loud even I heard it.

Fighting to contain my emotions, I dug my bleeding fingers into the sludge and began our 1000 yard journey...

"Sir, Sir!"

I heard the gruff voice of authority in the distance. I returned to my mental fog and continued to march forward. Now, where was I? Ahhh, yes... memories of military school... hazing... crawling in the mud.

"SIR, SIR!"

There it was again. Even louder Who was it? What does he want? Is he talking to me?

I shook my head to clear the fog. I tried to get my bearings. I was walking up a steep, winding mountain pass... I was in some foreign country... but was in too much pain to really care which one.

"Sir, you need to slow down!" Sergeant Reynolds grabbed me by the arm and forced me to stop. As he pulled me aside for a private conference in the middle of the rocky mountain path, I noticed the large beads of sweat rolling from his flushed face.

"Sergeant, you don't look too good." I chuckled as he pulled me away from the soldiers toward the front of the formation. "Are you having trouble keeping up?"

"This is serious, Sir. We have to slow down!"

"Okay, Sergeant, who is falling behind? We have trained for months. Everyone should be ready. Is there an injury? I am keeping the pace. Bring me the section leader of the soldier who is holding us back."

"No, no, no, Sir!"

"What do you mean, 'no'?" This isn't like you, Mike, so tell me what's going on here?"

"Sir, it's Alpha Company."

"What about 'em?" I inquired.

Sergeant Reynolds whispered, "They are behind us... er ...well they are supposed to be anyway."

"I don't care, Mike. Captain Smith doesn't know how to train his people. I'm not going to let that prima donna hold us back. March on!"

"Sir!" Sergeant Reynolds exclaimed. "The Colonel is with Alpha!"

"Hey, sergeant, you have a wonderful idea there! Why don't we give the men a 20 minute break? It will give me a chance to check everyone out. I'll start at the front and you can work up from the back. Keep an eye on Private

Childers. I think he started to limp about two miles back, but he won't admit it."

"Will do, Sir. How are your injuries holding up? The doctor said you shouldn't even be here!"

"I'll be fine, just check out the men. We only have 16 miles left to go tonight."

As I looked down at the bulging leather of my boots, I was reminded of the stress fractures in my feet. This was only overshadowed by the throbbing emanating from my left ankle which I had twisted by stepping on a loose rock eight miles earlier.

We marched on through the night... I don't remember much because I was on the brink of passing out from the pain most of the time. I just remember telling myself that I couldn't let my men see me fail. As their leader, they depended on me to be the beacon of hope.

In my pain, I thought of Vice Admiral James Bond Stockdale who was one of the most highly decorated officers in the history of the US Navy.

In his book, *Good to Great*, Jim Collins relates how Stockdale described his coping strategy during his period in the Vietnamese POW camp. Everyone knows about John McCain's years as a POW, but few know about Stockdale's heroism.

"I never lost faith in the end of the story, I never doubted not only that I would get out, but also that I would prevail in the end and turn the experience into the defining event of my life, which, in retrospect, I would not trade."

When Collins asked who didn't make it out, Stockdale replied:

"Oh, that's easy, the optimists. Oh, they were the ones who said, 'We're going to be out by Christmas.' And Christmas would come, and Christmas would go. Then they'd say, 'We're going to be out by Easter.' And Easter would come, and Easter would go. And then Thanksgiving, and then it would be Christmas again. And they died of a broken heart."

Witnessing this philosophy of duality, Collins went on to describe it as the **Stockdale Paradox**:

> *"You must never confuse faith that you will prevail in the end — which you can never afford to lose — with the discipline to confront the most brutal facts of your current reality, whatever they might be."*

I guess it's kind of a badge of pride to say I completed a marathon in the mountains of Korea in full combat gear with fractured feet... but I don't know if it was worth the price.

When we finally made it back to camp, I collapsed behind a tree... away from my soldiers and hidden from the ambulance that was waiting for us (lots of people were injured that night). I passed out and woke up 16 hours later in the same spot.

My feet were so swollen that I couldn't get my boots off and I couldn't walk. I crawled half a mile to my barracks...

with my full combat load. I had sustained permanent damage to my feet legs and back. Like I said earlier, it takes a lot to win. But I still believe it is costlier to lose.

Unable to perform in combat any longer, I was then transferred to a staff position at brigade headquarters. What I thought would be a boring "walk in the park" ended up being one of the most incredible management experiences I have ever faced (to this day).

Shortly after my reassignment, we entered monsoon season. It rained... and rained... and rained. As it turns out, it hadn't rained that much in more than 50... or was it 100? ... years. The rivers swelled, and then overflowed. As the ground became oversaturated, mud began sliding down hills all around us.

Cars, buildings, houses... you name it - started sliding down the mountains all around us. I knew it was bad when I saw a railroad car we used to store TOW missiles in... float away... right in front of my barracks.

As the flood waters rose, the rain continued. Bad became worse as landmines and unexploded bombs left over from the Korean War became exposed all around us. Thousands died. Millions were homeless.

It was declared a national disaster area, to say the least. Everyone was running around like headless chickens. No phones, no electricity, no plumbing, no roads... no FEMA (not that FEMA would have helped).

We were severely understaffed at the HQ as it was. Our brigade was stretched out all over the country and my boss (the colonel) had to jump in a chopper and take care of a million things... general's orders.

I'll give you three guesses who was left in charge. Yup, you guessed it... yeah, this young, limping infantry officer. Now, that's the most extreme case of on-the-job training I have ever experienced.

Half of our camp was under water. All the roads were completely impassable. I had 5,000 troops with nowhere to go and a lot of them were now homeless. Our camp had sustained over $5 BILLION worth of damage. Phone communications were completely out and radio was spotty at best.

This is where I learned the power of a team. We had some of the most capable soldiers and officers there (yes, many officers outranked me, but they were concerned with their own subordinate units... leaving me to coordinate the activities of all 5,000 of us).

Knowing that I knew nothing (in the training world we call that conscious incompetence), I assembled a crack team of delegates from each of the subordinate units. I had two people representing each unit on call, 24 hours a day. One would always stay at the HQ and the other was a runner.

I held status meetings at least twice a day with all of the senior leadership. I learned just to call the meetings and structure them... then get out of the way and let the smart people do their thing. I facilitated problem solving between the officers and NCO's (noncommissioned officers) without even hinting that I had any authority (because in many ways I really didn't).

By facilitating effective problem solving, brainstorming, and communication, we were able to leverage 110% of our resources. How can that be, you ask? We discovered an Air Force unit close by that everyone was ignoring. When we found out they had a couple bulldozers... we put them to work right away!

Through teamwork, we were able to accomplish so much more than operating alone. We had set a momentum that carried us through the recovery effort. After only four weeks, our camp was rated as 90% operational. The guys next door (with more than two times the resources and an in-tact leadership team) were only 40% operational during the same timeframe. In fact, they weren't even at 80% operational after eight weeks.

The lesson here? Utilize every resource at your disposal, and create teams where ever possible. Eight individual horses cannot pull a wagon, but harness them together and they become a strong force that can move tons, even tons of mud.

My injuries eventually lead to an honorable medical discharge. I don't feel the pain so much anymore, just on long runs or when I have to be on my feet all day.

After having to complete a mission when everything is life and death, even the big, international projects I tackle today seem surprisingly simple.

With the right commitment, focus and energy, even the impossible can be made possible.

Let me tell you about an incredible consulting team I was part of that did just that.

The client company had just spun off a major international corporation. I'd be more specific, but as you will soon see... I must respect client confidentiality (and maintain the anonymity of the corporate clowns).

This company had freed itself from the large, cumbersome, international bureaucracy, and was now expected to be quick, nimble, and innovative... but the ideas and new product innovations just weren't coming. The big corporate culture had not gone away and people were still spending more time complaining about being stagnant than doing something about it.

You know the types. Sitting around in the break room, whining about how nothing was happening, instead of being on their feet *making* things happen.

In the past, when they were just a division of a large company, they could depend on others to support them during the not-so-innovative times. There was enough bureaucracy to mask inefficiency; always somebody else to blame. Now that they were on their own, they needed to bring home the bacon on a daily basis. (Too bad none of them had served in Congress. They would have known how to bring home pork, but I digress...) Management wanted to see results and there was no where to hide.

They needed to move fast. Not only did the culture need to change... they needed tangible innovations to fill a very lean product pipeline.

I gotta respect the company for what they did... They called in our "dream team" of strategic innovation experts. They had to trust us, take our recommendations, and execute. No time to do an 18 month analysis of the plan. They needed to take some calculated risks, more internal-political than anything else.

Why?

The employees were sick of failed new initiatives with the new company. Sick of talk without action. Sick of promises. Sick of everything.

We needed to not only motivate these guys, but also tap into their brains, empower them and get them moving into action.

From idea to completion, we helped turn the company's innovation draught around in less than two months.

We planned a 'round the world' Strategic Innovation tour where we held events at major facilities in Europe, Asia, and the United States.

We gathered managers, engineers, scientists, and business strategists... about three hundred of them - into closed door strategic brainstorming sessions. All participants were treated as "equal minds" as we guided them through three, three-day sessions where we used the most innovative and cutting edge idea generation techniques in the most amazing mastermind process I have ever witnessed.

The result?

I'd say pretty good… When all was said and done, we calculated roughly… 12,735 business ideas… give or take.

We didn't have time to evaluate the business value of all of them… our breakout teams were only able to take a cursory examination of about 2,973 of the ideas. Those ideas alone carried a financial projection of over…

$$$ TWO BILLION DOLLARS $$$

The best part is… they actually followed through with many of the ideas. The day after we left, they had days and days of closed door sessions with their patent attorneys to make sure they followed up with and got moving on every marketable idea.

These guys were smart enough to know that $2 billion worth of ideas is worthless without implementation.

I must admit the day we calculated the totals… well, that was a great day. I genuinely hope the management didn't sit back and bask in their accomplishments and expect a few days of mental effort to fix all their lifelong problems.

Success is not a single destination - it's an ongoing effort.

Success is a moving target.

The day you think you have arrived is the day you begin to lose. Sorry folks, but there will always be one more book to read, one more seminar to attend, one more coaching session to better your skills and abilities.

Your competition is doing it... does that tell you something? To stay ahead, not only must you stay focused, but you need to be better, faster, smarter and provide more value than the "other guy."

Perhaps you have noticed something in this book that is missing. What do I obviously avoid that most strategy books focus almost entirely on?

YOUR OPPONENT!

Fact is... nine times out of ten, you are your own worst enemy and you cause your own destruction before you even face literal opposition. The worst part is, just as many people fall victim to their successes and not just their failures.

Yes, I do share a story where I was totally hosed over by one guy, but if I had been a little more aware of my surroundings, a little more alert, I could have managed the situation better. ...but there you have it. I had a bad situation and I learned from it. I moved on.

People are so concerned with the other guy in business... in life... in everything - that they fail to really develop their own strategy and objectives.

Personal and organizational development should be the cornerstone of your strategy. Celebrate your victories, but don't rest on your laurels. The saying, "Pride comes before a fall" has more truth than people care to recognize.

As part of my intense military school indoctrination, I was forced to memorize Latin phrases and several pages of text... much of which stays with me to this day. One phrase that continually rings through my ears is:

Sic transit gloria mundi

It is a Latin phrase that means "Thus passes the glory of the world." It has been interpreted as "Fame is fleeting." One of the more famous versions was attributed to the famous WWII general, George C. Patton. He said:

For over a thousand years Roman conquerors returning from the wars enjoyed the honor of triumph, a tumultuous parade. In the procession came trumpeters, musicians and strange animals from conquered territories, together with carts laden with treasure and captured armaments. The conquerors rode in a triumphal chariot, the dazed prisoners walking in chains before him. Sometimes his children robed in white stood with him in the chariot or rode the trace horses. A slave stood behind the conqueror holding a golden crown and whispering in his ear a warning: that all glory is fleeting.

Don't allow your glory to be fleeting.

Your 60 Second Strategy:

Get It Done

By

- Making a decision and acting on it RIGHT AWAY

- Continuing to work towards long term goals, even when faced with multiple setbacks and failures. . . Keep at it.

- Treating your energy as valuable currency and spending it only on executing tasks that will produce long term results

- Following through with plans once they have been set

- Concentrating your resources and energy with the speed and intensity of a laser light

- Monitoring your plan and adapting when necessary

- Taking smart risks and moving on them decisively

- Rewarding yourself and having some fun along the way

- Maintaining your focus on the prize and not getting derailed by minor setbacks and distractions

- Remembering that perseverance is the most important factor for success

DO THIS NOW

1. Go to **www.60secondStrategist.com** and download the *Get It Done worksheets* and bonus chapters.

2. Think of someone who can benefit from this book.

3. Pass this book on to the person identified in step 2.

4. Launch your plan NOW! GO! GO! GO!

Conclusion

"Watch your thoughts, for they become words.
Watch your words, for they become actions.
Watch your actions, for they become habits.
Watch your habits, for they become character.
Watch your character, for it becomes your destiny."
-Frank Outlaw

Okay, so now we have reached the end of this book and the beginning of your new journey.

Some of you may still be thinking, "Wait! I don't get it! No flowchart? No algorithm? No map of how to solve my problems in 60 seconds?"

Nope.

Let me try to explain.

When a car crash victim is rushed into the ER, do you think the doctors pull out a flowchart or a map that tells them what to do? Do you really think you can contain that knowledge in their heads inside a single chart? How about 100 charts? The truth is, you can't fit their knowledge into a book or even a stack of books.

You are a human being... not a chart nor a book nor a machine. You are something much more significant... something much more complex - a learning, growing creature made in the image of God. Contained within this book are some exercises to help you build a foundation for streamlining and speeding up your decision making ability and capacity for action.

Within the stories, I have embedded 60 strategic principles for you to experience... this is plenty for you to cogitate on for the next ten years or so. If you can master all of these, you have mastered strategy, and most likely life as well. When you work on these skills, combined with what you already know, you will begin to think faster, learn faster and execute faster.

That's the magic of the system. You just have to do... to act... to implement.

I have also included an ever-growing set of tools and resources on the website:

www.60secondStrategist.com

These tools will help you as you learn to manage your business and your life faster and better.

You will also find additional useful coaching tools at:

www.SixtySigma.com

It is my hope that you found my stories interesting and were also able to extract the nuggets of wisdom from them and... well, I hope you were able to think about ways to apply this stuff to your own business and your own life. But just in case you still don't get it...

Are you still asking yourself, "What's with the stories? Where is my explicit checklist?"

All I can do is give you a quote from my #1 mentor and life coach... and pray that this will all sink in and help you improve every aspect of your life:

His disciples came and asked him, "Why do you use parables when you talk to the people?"

He replied, "You are permitted to understand the secrets of the Kingdom of Heaven, but others are not. To those who listen to my teaching, more understanding will be given, and they will have an abundance of knowledge. But for those who are not listening, even what little understanding they have will be taken away from them. That is why I use these parables. For they look, but they don't really see. They hear, but they don't really listen or understand.

This fulfills the prophecy of Isaiah that says:

**'When you hear what I say,
you will not understand.
When you see what I do,
you will not comprehend.
For the hearts of these people are hardened,
and their ears cannot hear,
and they have closed their eyes—
so their eyes cannot see,
and their ears cannot hear,
and their hearts cannot understand,
and they cannot turn to me
and let me heal them.'**

Even if faith plays no part in your life, you may learn from what Jesus went on to say:

"But blessed are your eyes, because they see; and your ears, because they hear. I tell you the truth, many prophets and righteous people longed to see what you see, but they didn't see it. And they longed to hear what you hear, but they didn't hear it." Matthew 13:10-17

And finally, if you were wondering about our Miracle Baby ...Elizabeth Grace was born at a very solid 7 lbs. 5 oz. and 19 ½ inches. We had some complications that were a little scary at the time, but she's fine now and 100% healthy. She was absolutely perfect for her first year of life... then someone told her she was two and reminded her she was human and not an angelic creation. So now we have four normal, yet very beautiful and amazing children; we are truly blessed.

Today Leslie is doing extremely well and has recovered nicely from her pregnancy. We have had au pairs and nannies come and go in a valiant effort to help her out with the four kids, but we have found that in our family anyway, parenting is best left for the parents. Leslie dreams of taking her Twenty Million Angels ... an organization dedicated to raising disability awareness... to the national level, but her responsibilities as an executive officer of Sixty Sigma Inc, as well as her (much more important) job as CEM (Chief Executive Mommy) take precedence right now. If you go to www.twentymillionangels.org and see a website there, you know that things are plugging along. If nothing's there... it means she's still plugging away.

And as for that jackass of a boss I had that nearly destroyed me, he ran into some problems with corporate shenanigans a year or so after I left the company. I made millions in my own consulting firm and he died penniless. Right after he got hit by a bus. Thought you'd want to know. Karma, cosmic justice, or angelic intervention, you decide. Just kidding. He did actually kinda go berserk after what I like to think of as "the incident"... he quit coming into work, except on rare occasions... then he suddenly announced he'd gotten a job on the west coast and took off, leaving virtually everything behind. I mean, he didn't even clear out his office at all. He had trophies, plaques, sales and marketing awards, framed pictures..... he just left it all behind. Ashamed maybe? Be nice to think so.

And finally finally (really, I mean it this time), a closing thought from Mark Twain:

"I am opposed to millionaires, but it would be dangerous to offer me the position."

Wishing you a 'dangerous position' and all good fortune in every endeavor,

Tony G
Your 60 Second Strategy Coach

About the Author

Tony Galliano is an author, speaker, strategy consultant and executive coach.

He is the president of Sixty Sigma Inc. Proudly Located in Chicago's John Hancock Tower, along the Magnificent Mile, Sixty Sigma specializes in helping teams from Fortune 500 Companies, small businesses, government agencies and non-profit organizations achieve breakthrough performance through strategic thinking.

Tony's methodology is based on extensive research on thinking and the brain. Multiple applications of 60 Second Strategist concepts are designed to dramatically improve creativity, strategic thinking, problem solving, management, leadership, teaching, learning, self-understanding, communication and team development. Tony seeks to apply 60 Second Strategist principles to his varied responsibilities: from coaching, to consulting, day-to-day operations, to sales, to workshop design and presentations.

Having spent millions of client dollars and years of his life in the development of innovation, leadership, and marketing curriculum, Tony now brings this knowledge to his clients. His advice has been spread around the world through work with hundreds of organizations including Fortune 500, governments, royal families, entrepreneurs and non-profits.

Tony's personal goal is to promote a better understanding of how individuals and organizations think and become more strategic as well as to enhance learning and communication technologies worldwide through the application and development of the 60 Second Strategist concept. Sixty Sigma Inc. with affiliates worldwide continues to research and develop products and applications in the fields of strategic thinking and business strategy.

www.ingramcontent.com/pod-product-compliance
Lightning Source LLC
Chambersburg PA
CBHW021953170526
45157CB00003B/971